Winning

SUNY Series in International Management

Andrzej K. Kozminski, Patricia Sanders, and Sarah Sanderson King, editors

Winning

Continuous Improvement Theory in High-Performance Organizations

Krzysztof Obloj
Donald P. Cushman
Andrzej K. Kozminski

State University of New York Press

658.3
Obₗ ω

Published by
State University of New York Press

© 1995 State University of New York

All rights reserved

Printed in the United States of America

No part of this book may be used or reproduced in any manner
whatsoever without written permission. No part of this book may
be stored in a retrieval system or transmitted in any form or by
any means including electronic, electrostatic, magnetic tape,
mechanical, photocopying, recording, or otherwise without the
prior permission in writing of the publisher.

For information address State University of New York Press, State
University Plaza, Albany, NY 12246

Production by Laura Starrett
Marketing by Dana Yanulavich

Library of Congress Cataloging in Publication Data

Obłój, Krzysztof.
  Winning : continuous improvement theory in high-performance
organizations / Krzysztof Obloj, Donald P. Cushman, Andrzej K.
Kozminski.
    p.   cm. — (SUNY series in international management)
  Includes bibliographical references (p.   ) and index.
  ISBN 0-7914-2521-5. — ISBN 0-7914-2522-3 (pbk.)
    1. Industrial productivity.   2. Labor productivity.   3. Work
groups.   4. Total quality management.   I. Cushman, Donald P.
II. Koźmiński, Andrzej K.   III. Title.   IV. Series.
HD56.025   1994
658.3'4—dc20   94-39616
                                                         CIP

10 9 8 7 6 5 4 3 2 1

Contents

List of Figures and Tables

Figures

Tables

A deep friendship and passionate love for another person is rooted in a common bond, an intimate caring, respect, and admiration for that other person. This book is dedicated to each of our significant others—Zofia, Sarah, Alicja—in celebration of three such unique relationships.

Preface

After a decade of research by universities, consulting firms, and organizational training divisions, we can conclude that organizations are having very limited success in employing various types of teamwork and continuous improvement programs. Studies conducted across industries and markets indicate that 70 percent of all such attempts fail to meet organizational expectations and that most continuous improvement programs are discontinued within two years of their introduction (*Economist* 1992:68–69; Fuchsberg 1992:B1; Tetzef 1992:12; Port, et al. 1992:66).

It is equally shocking to realize that while 70 percent of such programs fail to realize the expectations of firms that implement them, all of the firms leading their industry's category in the *Fortune* 500 survey report that teamwork, in the form of continuous improvement programs, is the primary reason for their success. Moreover firms like Intel, Motorola, and GE report between $1 billion and $500 million annual savings from such programs (Jacob 1993:67; Hillkirk 1989:10B).

Initially consultants and trainers cited several reasons for these discrepancies—lack of CEO commitment, customer focus, clear goals, link to financial payback, appropriate training, appropriate teamwork tools (Jacob 1993:66; Marbach 1993:93; Richey 1992:92). Only recently have empirical researchers begun to carefully document the underlying causes of these discrepancies (Port, et al. 1992:66–72; Stemple 1992).

First, there are major differences between high performance firms and all others in their learning ability. High performance firms, or firms with a return on assets of 7 percent or higher and a value added per employee of $74,000, could learn the use of all types of teamwork quickly and effectively while other firms could not (Port, et al. 1992:66–72).

Second, high performance firms had a full array of continuous improvement programs available; self-managed, cross-functional, benchmarking, outside linking, and breakthrough teams; and knew when to use each appropriately given the firm's overall strategy (Stemple 1992).

Third, high performance firms modified TQM teamwork patterns to fit a firm's corporate strategy and its monitoring and control systems (Rieley 1992).

This book attempts to illustrate how and when high performance firms employ a full range of continuous improvement programs to win the top ranking in their respective industries. In short, it seeks to teach us how to win through continuous improvement programs.

ONE

Competitive Advantage, Organizational Coalignment, and Strategy

> Top management must add value by enunciating the strategic architecture that guides the competence acquisition process. We believe an obsession with competence building will characterize the global winners of the 1990s. With the decade underway, the time for rethinking the concept of the corporation is already overdue. (Prahalad and Hamel, 1990: 91)

There are three major challenges facing organizations operating in today's violent and complex environment: environmental analysis, organizational analysis and strategic development.

Environmental Analysis. Every organization must configure its resources with regard to customers and competitors in such a way as to develop and sustain a competitive advantage. In a typical business environment organizational success involves a choice of competitive advantage that matches environmental contingencies and organizational competencies by providing a product/service which is notable for one of the following factors: low-cost, differentiation, product scope, or timing. These four sources of competitive advantage will be discussed in more detail below.

Organizational analysis. In order to sustain its advantage over time every organization must adapt to change and unpredictable threats. It must effectively configure its resources, capabilities, customers and competitors to respond to changing conditions. Maintaining its competitive positioning and continuously improving its organizational coalignment across the value chain rejuvenates a firm's competitive advantage in a changing environment. However, even the most successful organizations and managers must face the possibility that despite efforts to maintain a competitive posture, a disaster may strike, for example, rapid product obsolesce due to technological breakthrough, unexpected entry of new competitors, development of substitute products, or a swift decline in the market size. The exact nature of such a crisis is extremely difficult to predict. However, managers must be prepared for such eventualities.

Strategic Development. To sustain its advantage a successful organization must develop its *own* skills and knowledge. An organization must be able to learn from its experiences, and be able to differentiate between a) generic and publicly available knowledge gained over time, and b) tacit practical skills that yield a lasting and firm-specific advantage. The distinction between these two types of knowledge or skills is of crucial importance (Nelson 1990). Generic knowledge of technology or management can be patented or written down, or at least communicated and understood by those familiar with similar solutions. Generic knowledge of the company cannot remain its property for long, even if patents or secrecy delay its widespread application (Cantwell 1993). Tacit knowledge and skills are generated within an organization by individuals and teams as a complex outcome of its evolution and experience. These knowledge and skills are unique and almost impossible to copy directly, with similar effect, by other organizations. Therefore it is these skills that are crucial for an organization's competitive advantage and its lasting success in the market.

RELATED RESEARCH

Each of these three areas has attracted an extensive body of organizational research. A set of managerial solutions has been developed as tools for each area. Generally specific solutions have been developed for the various problems involved in each managerial challenge. The research focuses on the link between an organization and its competitors, producing such important concepts as competitive advantage, core competencies, and generic competitive strategies (Porter 1985, Prahalad and Hamel 1990, Porter 1980). Marketing studies have helped by developing a better understanding of the relationships among organizations, markets/products and customers (Deschamps and Nayak 1992). The growing body of literature dealing with tangible and intangible resources allows us to better understand the resource foundation of environmental and organizational analysis (Obloj and Joynt 1987; Itami and Roehl 1987; Grant 1991). The continuous development of organizational analysis has produced a tool known as "value chain analysis," which can be used for both functional and process investigation (Porter 1985; Cushman and King 1993; Cushman and King 1995). Organizational decline and crisis management research allows us to better understand the strengths and limitations of strategy, contingency planning and turnaround techniques (Hambrick and D'Aveni 1988; Meyer and Zucker 1989). The evolutionary economics approach by Nelson and Winter (1982) has led to a more coherent view of organizational evolution, learning and routines that embody the firm's localized and specific skills and competencies. The theory outlined in 1982 by Paul Romer modified the classical theory of growth, taking into account the importance of new ideas and practical, corporate knowledge about 'how to make things' (*The Economist*, January 4, 1992: 15).

A large volume of research and analysis still exists in different theoretical "pockets" that lack an integrating theoretical framework. Each pocket produces separate practical implications and tools, in effect forcing managers to deal with each problem separately under the general umbrella of the continuous improvement movement. It is our conviction that sufficient theoretical formulations and practical tools exist to develop an integrated framework of continuous improvement, the central question of which is simply, "How to become more successful?" Prior to entering into the main body of our theoretical analysis in Chapter 2, we will attempt to integrate the relationships among key themes arising from the literature dealing with the continuous improvement process. We shall explore (1) environment: the role of competitive advantage in a global, volatile and complex environment, (2) organizational value chain: the importance of coordination across organizational functions and processes, and (3) strategy: the basic linking pin between environmental and organizational resources. Strategy allows for the development of a system for environmental scanning, planned environmental linkages and the accumulation of practical, tacit knowledge.

ENVIRONMENTAL ANALYSIS AND
COMPETITIVE ADVANTAGE

> Success brings on imitators, who respond with superior features, lower prices, or some new way to draw customers away. Time, the denominator of economic value, eventually renders nearly all advantages obsolete. (Williams, 1992: 29)

Every firm that wants to operate successfully in a competitive environment must develop some source of competitive advantage to help satisfy its customers' needs. Strategic management literature suggests four generic sources of product competitive advantage: cost, differentiation, focus and time (Porter 1985; Cushman and King, 1992, 1995).

Four Sources of Competitive Advantage

Cost.   A company can develop an overall cost advantage in various ways, such as by exploiting favorable environmental conditions (for example, access to cheap resources), developing efficient-scale facilities, maintaining tight control over fixed and variable costs, and intelligently cutting the costs of organizational activities. The essence of this cost-cutting drive is simple: to maintain lower costs than those of market rivals while offering goods/services of comparable value to the customer. Well-known examples include Japanese automakers (for example, Toyota, Honda, Mazda, Mitsubishi), earth-moving equipment managers (Komatsu), and electronic consumer goods producers

(Sony, JVC), which have consistently produced higher value goods at lower unit costs that comparable American and European manufacturers.

Differentiation. A company can gain a competitive advantage through product differentiation by creating products/services with at least one feature perceived as unique by customers. The possibilities for product differentiation are practically unlimited and can be observed in all types of industries along many dimensions. Examples include user-friendly software (Apple Computers), advanced engineering (Mercedes automobiles), unusual design (Bang & Olufsen hi-fi equipment), reliable appliances (Maytag, Electrolux), and trustworthy service (L.L. Bean). The essential feature of a product differentiation strategy lies in the development of brand loyalty and low price sensitivity by customers.

Product Line Scope. A company can achieve a competitive advantage based on the scope of the product offering in two ways. One method is through a broader range of products/services than that offered by competitors. General Motors provides its customers worldwide with small, medium, large, luxury, and sport cars; station wagons; minivans; pick-ups and trucks, thus creating a competitive advantage based on a wide product and market scope. The second method for achieving a scope competitive advantage is through a steady focus on limited markets/products, aiming for perfection in those segments. For example, Volvo concentrates only on sedans, station wagons, and trucks. Classic examples of a narrow focus competitive advantage are marketing niches developed by Rolls-Royce or Lamborghini in cars; Philip-Patek, Blancpain and Rolex in watches; and H. Rubinstein in cosmetics. The focused scope of these producers made their brands status symbols.

Time to Market. A firm may gain a competitive advantage by managing time better than its competitors. Joseph Schumpeter, a noted economist, discussed this source of competitive advantage many years ago. He wrote on the advantage enjoyed by a classical innovator who was the first to market with a product. Cushman and King (1993) call this form of advantage high-speed management. Examples include Apple Corporation's development, production and marketing of user-friendly, personal computers; Chrysler Corporation's mini-vans; and Sony's development of the Walkman. These firms all beat potential competitors to market, capturing large market shares and high profits, and enhancing their respective brand image.

While all firms in today's market are seeking an opportunity to master at least one of the generic sources of competitive advantage, it is important to stress that the choice of effective competitive advantage is not absolute. It depends upon the unique dynamic created by the behavior of customers and competitors' tactics. Let us review the major customer and competitive trends that are developing in the market and their influence on the development of a competitive advantage.

Consumer and Competitor Environmental Trends

Customers.   Today's markets are characterized by quick market saturation, a shrinking product life cycle, convergence of customers' tastes and needs, and volatility in market segments and niches.

Quick market saturation and a shrinking product life cycle are related but distinct phenomena. Market saturation results from the practice of rapid imitation by both traditional competitors and new entrants as long as the proprietary technology and patents can be broken, bypassed or exploited in unexpected ways. Quick market saturation of the PC market around the world resulted from the development of cheap clones and new sales tactics. The latter are especially visible in the U.S. where mail-order companies such as Gateway 2000, Packard Bell, Dell and other firms flood the market with cheap clones. Saturation of the PC market has made customers discriminating and corporations vulnerable. In the June, 1990 issue of *Computer Shopper*, 129 companies advertised personal computers. The following year 135 firms advertised in the June 1991 issue. However, only 65 of them appeared in the two consecutive years (Kupfer 1991: 120).

Shrinking life cycles result from the speed of technological and marketing innovations generating new products and services. The duration of the lifecycle in different markets varies, (for example, in Japan's soft drink market over 1,000 new products are introduced each year!). However, most markets exhibit a clear trend of shrinking product life cycles. The unprecedented speeding up of product life cycles in the computer and car markets is a warning to slower, revolving markets.

The global convergence of consumers' tastes and needs is a second important global trend caused by the increasing predominance of market economies, the wide-reaching distribution of international brands, and a high-speed telecommunications network spreading information about common customer needs and tastes.

The recent (1992) opening of Disneyland near Paris, France, precipitated a bitter public debate on the dominance of American consumer values and tastes in Europe. Many companies, (for example, Wrigley and Gillette) entering the markets of Poland, the Czech Republic, Slovakia, and the former Soviet Union are merely dubbing their international ads without adaptation. Companies have not needed to localize the creative aspect of their advertising efforts because consumer preferences in East European markets are similar to consumer preferences elsewhere in the world. However, a growing homogeneity of the needs and tastes in different markets coexists with increasing product volatility.

Increasing product volatility is caused by the complex and dynamic nature of the consumer-product dynamic. Consumers' needs and tastes are changing. Those changes have become more subtle and dynamic. As a result the traditional segmentation of markets is becoming obsolete and being replaced by interlocking "slices." Representative of this trend is the car market. For decades the American car market has been split into the five major socioeconomic segments developed in the late twentieth century by Alfred Sloan of General Motors. However, during the 1980s, customers' needs and tastes were increasingly redefined. Different lifestyles, values and expectations function as basic variables, slicing the market in hundreds of ways and destabilizing traditional market segments (Drucker 1991: 173).

Competitors

The competitive environment is characterized by increasing hostility, growing complexity and a quickening rate of change.

The essence of hostile competition in the main domestic and global markets is a drive to eliminate competitors by resorting to cost cutting, increased differentiation, and higher speeds of product improvement and replacement. This increasingly aggressive type of competition characterizes a company searching for any type of competitive advantage in order to dominate its competitors through increased market shares and profitability.

The complexity of competition is characterized by several factors. First, the large number of competitors in major markets is changing rapidly, making traditional economic models of stable oligopolistic competition obsolete. Second, the industrial products, consumer products, and financial and futures markets are connected in increasingly sophisticated ways. The competitive position of a company may be determined by the cost and quality of its products, but the possibility of buying in the futures markets and financial hedging of future deliveries complicates competitive positioning. Third, the complexity of competition is affected by the increasing number of stake-holders regulating markets either directly or indirectly. Often these stakeholders, such as governmental agencies, interest groups, and participants in the distribution channel, make competition much less predictable.

The high speed of change in the market is a converging push and pull result of pressure from consumers and efforts made by competitors. The development of consumer needs (for example, a lasting need for more powerful PCs) drives the introduction of endless improvements to existing products. The efforts to leapfrog the competition result in inventions like the Chrysler minivan, the Hewlett-Packard laserprinter, and Goodyear's Aquatred tire.

ENVIRONMENTAL TRENDS AND COMPETITIVE ADVANTAGE

These market trends on the part of both consumers and competitors converge and influence the search for competitive advantage in the following ways:

Duration.   Every competitive advantage, regardless of its nature, is only temporary. Its foundation can be destroyed by competitive dynamics and/or consumer behavior. This means that managers must constantly analyze and isolate or upgrade the firm's competitive advantage.

Complexity.   Companies must match the complex and volatile nature of markets with equally complex and adaptive strategies to upgrade their competitive advantage. Companies anchoring their competitive advantage simultaneously in low cost, differentiated product quality and focus, and high-speed adaptation are better off than their competitors who are missing one of these elements.

Consistency. The complexity of competitive advantage combined with the need for its adaptation means that the process of rejuvenating competitive advantage cannot be performed in random ways through an occasional burst of managerial energy. The volatile and complex nature of the business environment implies a need for a systematic approach to analyzing the structural and dynamic sources of potential advantage (Cavaleri and Obloj 1993).

AN ORGANIZATION AS A
COMPLEX VALUE CHAIN

A useful way to analyze an organization is as a set of activities called a "value chain." We will discuss in more detail the value chain concept developed by Porter (1985) in Chapter 6, as we define coalignment. However, we will now begin with three perspectives inherent in the value chain: functional, process and extended. We will identify how these analytical perspectives help to define the potential sources of organizational competitive advantage.

Functional Perspective

A functional perspective of the value chain views the organization as a system of two main activity types: line (primary) and staff (support).[1] The main feature of line activities is their direct involvement in transforming inputs into outputs. Line activities are mainly "energy-processing" activities (for example, storing, manufacturing, and transporting). In contrast, staff activities are primarily "information-processing" activities (accounting, training, research and development).

Such an approach to organization can be useful, as it draws scholars' and managers' attention to the clear, functionally-based differences as a potential source of competitive advantage. A firm can gain an advantage over its competitors due to relative excellence of some primary activities. These primary activities are in turn dependent on organizational resources and practical skills embodied in some functions of the staff activities. For example, the competitive advantage of such corporations as Xerox and Polaroid depended for many years on well-defended proprietary technology. A competitive advantage can also be derived directly from the support activities, for example, speed of information processing and new product development as demonstrated with Intel microprocessors or in the skillful management of supplier relations, as demonstrated by the Mark and Spencers retail chain.

Business Process Perspective

An organization can be analyzed in a more dynamic fashion as a series of processes. This approach calls for identifying potential sources of competitive advantage in the interrelations of different functional activities. The performance of various functional activities influences the efficiency of other activities; thus, a real competitive advantage must be sought in those organizational processes that spread across an organization, that is, product R&D, production processes, and sales and customer service.

The business process perspective of the value chain combines discrete functions into overlapping business processes and maintains that process can become an outstanding capability and therefore a source of competitive advantage. For example, in the pharmaceutical industry, Merck dominates its competitors due to superior research and development, which results in a stream of innovative drugs, while Glaxo International's excels in effecting short drug approval times and innovative sales methods throughout the world.

Vital to developing a competitive advantage through business process analysis is understanding how various elements of an organization interact in continuous process. However, in the volatile and complex business environment, such an analysis must be extended into larger industrial structures and markets and reach out into the organization's environment (Porter 1985; Rockart and Short 1989; Cushman and King, 1992, 1995; Cavaleri and Obloj 1993).

Extended Perspective

An analysis of the organization as an open system that includes its suppliers, uses, competitors, and other stakeholders, for example, government agencies, has been advocated since the 1970s; however, it is recently gaining significance due to three primary factors.

The pace of market development (notably in pharmaceuticals, chemicals, semiconductors, microprocessors, computers, and food production) quickly makes the knowledge and technology accumulated by organizations obsolete. Therefore organizations must constantly scan the environment and coalign with suppliers, competitors and customers. Linkages with suppliers allow for increased cost control, while coaligning with customers assures timely information on current needs, expectations, and limitations. Alliances with competitors allows the sharing of costs of both adaptations and innovations.

The complexity of changes fueled by technological developments, substitutes, and changing market segments demands a corresponding complex network of linkages. Therefore, organizations' alliances are more commonly transgressing traditional industrial boundaries and increasing the overall number of linkages.

The intensity of global competition and practice of benchmarking speeds up imitations of and improvements on functional- and process-based competitive advantages.

While it can be argued that these three causes are not equally strong in all markets, a combined effect is clear: functional and process-based advantages are and will be increasingly difficult to sustain. Therefore the external coalignment seen in negotiated linkages with major stakeholders in the environment, as well as resulting processes, are quickly becoming the third source of competitive advantage that world class competitors are probing and developing.

Conclusions

Let us summarize the discussion of an organization as a value chain up to this point. We clarified the three potential sources of competitive advantage as identified through value chain analysis: (1) functional activities, utilizing the best of organizational resources; (2) organizational processes, building unique or at least better capabilities than those of competitors; and (3) linkages with the environment that allow for the expansion, refinement, and improvement of organizational capabilities. These are different but interrelated sources of competitive advantage with one common dominant theme.

A sustainable competitive advantage can be achieved only by effectively matching the functions and processes across the organization with the configuration of the environment as defined by suppliers, customers, and competitors. Value chain analysis is a tool for the continuous search for improved external and internal coalignment leading to a competitive advantage. To compete effectively in the market, management must develop a strategy encompassing the company's competitive advantage.

STRATEGY: A LINKING PIN

A firm's ability to stay viable, that is, to earn a profit in excess of its cost of capital, depends upon two factors: industry attractiveness and individual company strategy. The first factor, the attractiveness of the environment (industry) in which a company is positioned, has been traditionally stressed by economists. The industry attractiveness factor, part of the economic theory of the firm, has recently lost some of its predictive and explanatory power. Empirical research has failed to support the direct relation between a firm's profitability and its industrial environment (Rumelt 1987; Porter 1991). Variance components analysis to rates of return on capital performed by R. Rumelt (1987: 141) illustrates the weak correlation.

Table 1.1 Results of Variance Components Analysis of Return on Capital, 1,292 U.S. Corporations

	INDUSTRY DEFINITION	
	3-DIGIT	4-DIGIT
Variance due to industry effects	3.9	4.7
Variance due to firm effects within industries	19.2	17.6

Source: Rumelt, R. 1987, Theory, Strategy, and Entrepreneurship, In: Teece, D. J. (ed), *The Competitive Challenge*, New York, Harper and Row: 141

According to Rumelt (1987: 141), "The data show that the variance in long-run profitability within industries is three to five times larger than the variance across industries. Clearly, the important sources of excess (or subnormal) profitability in this data set were firm-specific rather than the results of industry membership."

The second factor, a company strategy superior to that of its competitors, is traditionally stressed by management theory. Strategy should link organizational functions and processes with the environment in such a way as to secure a sustainable competitive advantage for the firm. This means that an organization must (1) obtain and utilize its tangible resources and develop intangible resources to ensure higher efficiency and effectiveness than its competitors, and (2) manage processes of product development, production, and marketing better than its competitors, while (3) negotiating favorable linkages with all important stakeholders in the environment. The framework of this complex process is shown in Figure 1.1.

At the highest theoretical level we have a generic problem central to all successful organizational strategies: "What to improve?" The answer to this question must take into consideration two major questions that reside at the next level: 1) How to compete? 2) Where to compete? Moving to the third theoretical level in Figure 1.1, we have the problem of how to develop an organizational competitive advantage of cost, differentiation, scope, or time within a certain environment. Value chain analysis is the best approach to attack this problem. The distinction among functional, business process, and extended value chain perspectives allows us to concentrate on three drivers of competitive advantage explaining the fit between environment and competitive advantage: organizational capabilities and resources and linkages. Let us turn our attention to defining and strategically identifying resources and capabilities. An analysis of linkages appears in following chapters.

Resources and Capabilities Defined

Resources are basic inputs to business activities. The typical resources of the firm include financial and human resources, physical facilities, product and process technologies, brands, patents and general know-how. The strategic impor-

Figure 1.1

Basic Links Among Strategy, Environment, and Competitive Advantage

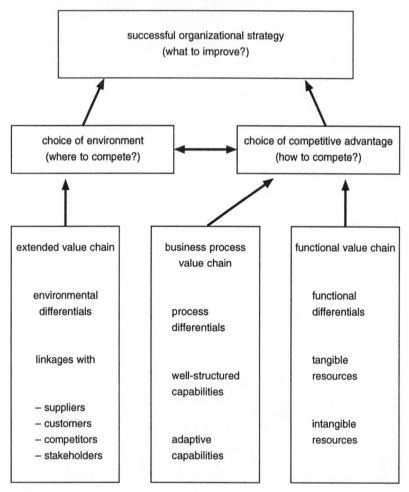

tance of intangible resources differs from that of tangible resources (Hall 1992). Intangible resources such as brand names, copyrights and patents, know-how, and so forth are more durable and more difficult to identify and replicate than tangible assets. Thus, a strategic advantage that exploits intangible assets is more difficult for competitors to copy and more recognizable to customers. Empirical research supports this assertion.

An exhaustive, longitudinal study (Hall 1992) of CEOs across British industrial sectors researched their perspective on the relative importance of intangible resources to overall company success. The analysis in Table 1.2 shows surprising unanimity over three major intangible resources: company reputation, product reputation and employee know-how. The relatively high ranking of supplier and distributor know-how indicates the importance of extended linkages with these groups.

The same study also shows that the replacement period for intangible resources is quite long. The three resources rated as the most important were also rated as the most durable, with an average of 10.8 years for company reputation, 6.0 years for product reputation, and 4.6 years for employee know-how (Hall 1992: 142).

For both tangible and intangible resources to enhance competitive advantage they must be combined in a meaningful way to create organizational capabilities.

Capabilities may be defined as the set of resources that are utilized in processes in a productive way (Grant 1991; Hall 1992).[2] Organizations perform in a cyclical manner. Over time, capabilities are molded either into standard, well-structured

Table 1.2 The Relative Importance of the Contribution Made by Intangible Resource to the Overall Success of the Business in 1987 and 1990

INTANGIBLE RESOURCE	RANKING*	
	1990	1987
Company Reputation	1	1
Product Reputation	2	2
Employee Know-How	3	3
Culture	4	5
Networks	5	4
Specialist Physical Resources	6	6
Data Bases	7	10
Supplier Know-How	8	7
Distributor Know-How	9	8
Public Knowledge	10	9

* 1: Most important, 10: Least important.

Source: Hall R. 1992. The Strategic Analysis of Intangible Resources, Strategic Management Journal, vol. 13, no. 2, p. 139

procedures or adaptive procedures (Cavaleri and Obloj 1993). The essence of standard procedures that effectively employ different sets of resources lies in their efficiency, simplicity, and repetitiveness, as in procedures of preventative maintenance, depositing a check, and dealing with customer complaints. The more stable the transformation process in an organization, the more appropriate are standardized procedures. The explanation of such a relationship takes three factors into account. First, standard procedures ensure the continuity of functional resources, for example, materials, finances, human inputs; the acquisition of resources and the regularity of operations. Second, standardization minimizes the cost of operations minimizing the necessary time, attention to, and sophistication of skills. Third, the stability of transformational processes allows for the accumulation of knowledge, through experience, about potentially disruptive events and the development of responsive procedures.

In addition to standard procedures, organizations develop adaptive procedures in cases for which the task is neither routine nor extremely complex. The essence of such adaptive capability is its degree of innovation. A typical example of such a procedure is new product development that incorporates various procedures such as recognizing customer needs, establishing an R&D budget, monitoring and evaluating prototypes, evaluating competitive products, running market tests, and so forth.

Having established definitions for and relations between resources and capabilities as a basis for strategy, we will now explore how these resources and capabilities are linked and managed in a systematic way, and identify the strategic sources of knowledge that help to utilize them effectively.

Strategic Identification of Resources

Utilizing a functional perspective helps in the identification and analysis of resources as inputs into the organizational functions and processes. Three strategic questions have theoretical and practical relevance for the identification of resources:

1. Can the company utilize fewer resources across different functional activities while supporting a similar volume of business? The answer lies in searching for low cost and/or scope

competitive advantages, as exercised by many aggressive acquirers, new management teams, and turnaround specialists. Economizing the use of resources involves some standard strategic moves, for example, limiting the number of products and the services offered, slashing inventory, cutting the workforce and selling equipment, spinning off some logistical activities, such as maintenance and transport, or merging functional department. For example, Chevron decided in 1992 to lower its costs by more than $60 million with two moves: (1) merging support activities across different business units and focusing technological development efforts, and (2) streamlining operations at the level of primary activities, mainly by trimming the workforce. ASEA Brown Boveri streamlines operations when acquiring a new company by laying off one-third of the employees working at the company headquarters. An important effect of such resource pruning is a cost advantage over competitors and a clear customer/competitor focus.

2. Can existing resources be used more effectively? Many competitive advantages are derived from strategies that dramatically increase the productivity of existing tangible and intangible resources. Probably the most commonly underdeveloped and under-utilized resource in American and European companies is human skills and abilities. Tapping these resources in an intensive way through quality circles enabled Japanese corporations to gain a decisive low cost–high quality competitive advantage and upgrade the qualifications of their workforce in the global markets of the 1980s. A dramatic example of increased productive exploitation of resources was the famous turnaround of the NUMMI factory. GM closed the factory in 1982 due to low productivity and quality, absenteeism, grievances, and drug and alcohol abuse. The plant reopened in 1984 with the same employees under Japanese management. Almost immediately, the NUMMI factory became a model for gains in productivity and quality achieved by a different approach to the same resources. The rigid GM hierarchical management system gave way to the empowerment of both managers and workers through team organization. The employees' skills were upgraded and fully utilized by job enrichment and rotation, while their problem-solving skills were simplified by pushing both competencies and responsibility down the line (Niland 1989). The same basic resource, employees' skills, was used in a different, more intensive way.

3. Do any resources need to be acquired? The functional analysis of resources might reveal that an organization does not have some crucial resources needed to develop a competitive advantage. Clinical examples of such situations can currently be found in Eastern European enterprises in Poland, Hungary, the Czech Republic, or Slovakia. Even though some of these firms have potential advantages due to a cheap, skilled labor-force and modern equipment, few can utilize the resources due to a lack of management expertise, especially in marketing and sales. Lack of management skills is literally breaking down entire strategies. To become competitive in world markets, these firms must either acquire knowledge and skills in the areas of marketing and sales (for example, by hiring Western managers or marketing agencies) or develop the skills internally.

Strategic Identification of Capabilities

In a most fundamental sense, companies have at their disposal similar resources: people, money, technology, facilities, and so forth, which are allocated to functions, processes, or linkages. But from a strategic point of view, organizations differ with respect to how efficiently and intensively they utilize those resources. Another major difference occurs in terms of how capabilities are spread across main processes of the value chain: product development, product delivery, and customer service. In the traditional consulting jargon, the best, highly utilized capabilities are called "organizational strengths." A company's strengths are defined relative to those of its competitors. To say that successful strategies should exploit strengths is a cliché of strategic management literature. McDonald's key success factor is its ability to transfer operational and managerial know-how and to achieve consistent levels of service in outlets around the world. Mercedes-Benz has been focused for years on perfecting its engineering and development process. Marks and Spencer is famous for its ability to establish a relationship with suppliers that ensures a high level of product quality. Coca-Cola's world-wide dominance on the soft-drink market can be attributed to a well-coordinated marketing effort. Toyota's main strengths were initially developed in the process of product delivery (low-cost cars) and more recently expanded to product development (differentiated Lexus model) and customer service.

Well-structured capabilities in one or all of the processes influence a firm's ability to attain product focus, low cost, and differentiation competitive advantages. These capabilities are directly related to the continuous improvement of every turn of the business cycle.

Adaptive capabilities influence a firm's ability to achieve a speed-competitive advantage. They relate to the innovative configuration of the resources within the processes. Benetton and Limited, apparel chains, link their stores with suppliers through innovative computer networks to speed up deliveries. Today's state-of-the-art, adaptive capabilities will likely become standard routines by the end of the decade. All automakers around the world are emulating the formerly innovative Japanese approach to product development by using cross-functional teams from the initial stages of product development. Jan Carlzon turned around the ailing Scandinavian Airline System in the 1980s by reconfiguring product delivery and service processes. Two innovative ideas for the service process involved establishing a new category of service called Euroclass and assigning to gate managers the responsibility for adherence to departure times. These moves established SAS's differentiation in the airline market. The process of product delivery was improved using self-managed and cross-functional teams that concentrated on 150 separate improvement projects spread over major organizational processes.

While some companies, such as 3M, which produces thousands of new or revised products annually, have made innovation their routine capability, most have not done so. Successful companies punctuate their routine operations with new and innovative procedures.

Strategic Identification of Sources of Knowledge

Linkages, resources, and capabilities are developed by organizational members using three main sources of knowledge: professional, technical, and practical.

Professional knowledge is a result of the general education process, which allows individuals to understand, memorize, and apply ideas, principles, and theories developed in different domains of science. Professional knowledge defines the basic ontological and epistemological assumptions and principles of rational conduct by allowing managers to build general frameworks for interpreting organizational problems in psychological, economic, political, and systemic ways.

Technical knowledge results from a specialized education process that enables an individual to understand how professional principles and assumptions are applied to processes. Technical knowledge helps in focusing on the description and explanation of tangible relations among an organization's inputs, transformation process and outputs and corresponding information flows. Processes of automated transport systems, robotics, and accounting are typical examples of applying technical knowledge.

Practical knowledge is developed from particular individual and team experience in the work place. In other words, practical knowledge is time- and place-specific, focusing on how to perform certain responsibilities effectively and under specific contingencies.

The three sources of knowledge that result from general, technical, and practical (on-the-job) education always overlap in real life. They all have their public and tacit components whose relation is relatively evident. While professional and technical knowledge is mainly public, practical knowledge, built upon case study analysis, is partially tacit and difficult to codify and transfer. Properly exploited practical knowledge enables organizations to build winning combinations of resources and capabilities.

CONCLUSIONS

This chapter's theoretical framework addresses the central question of the continuous improvement process: How to become more successful? We discussed the major premises and practical implications of complex and dynamic relationships between two major explanatory variables of successful strategic improvement: environment and competitive advantage. We addressed the major trends in today's business environment and the types of competitive advantage that organizations might pursue. Then we moved to answer the underlying question about principal drivers of proper adaptation of competitive advantage to environmental forces and trends. Our conclusion, based upon value chain analysis, was that these drivers include resources, capabilities, and external linkages. Professional, technical, and practical sources of knowledge must be exploited to develop such combinations of resources, capabilities, and linkages that can yield a sustainable competitive advantage.

Most treatments of management variables provide long lists that encourage intuitive analysis rather than providing managers with general principles to guide their decision making. To allow for more practical usage, we have set the stage for the investigation of the critical question: Why do some companies make their linkages, resources, and capabilities productive, improving them constantly, while others are unable to do so and are doomed to loose potential competitive advantages? The following chapters expand our theoretical framework and address more specific issues and theoretical answers pertinent to developing a theory of continuous improvement programs. The major thrust of our analysis will concentrate on five functions of the continuous improvement program: (1) negotiated linkages; (2) benchmarking; (3) cross-functional teams; (4) self-managed teams; and (5) breakthroughs. After establishing the components of our theory and outlining key relationships, we pursue a more detailed investigation in subsequent chapters by reviewing the existing literature, analyzing practical managerial experiences, and reviewing conclusions.

TWO

The Theory of Effective Continuous Improvement

> More and more of the world's goods
> require not the standardized and
> modest quality associated with mass
> production but continuous innova-
> tions and thus design and production
> changes and higher quality. Change
> and quality in turn require different
> organizational structures and work
> practices: decentralized structures,
> small-firm networks, or subcontrac-
> tors that are not dependent and
> exploited, and work practices in which
> conception and execution come
> together once more. Ch. Perrow (1992:
> 163)

In the last chapter we built two layers of a continuous improvement theory. The first layer dealt with the connections among
an organization's competitive advantage, reaction to a changing
environment, and ability to learn over time. Our analysis has
two main implications. First, the form and content of those
dynamic relations force any organization wanting to sustain its
competitive advantage to follow a continuous quest for improvement. Second, in a volatile environment where sources and
types of competitive advantage change, a program of improvement does not necessarily guarantee better performance than
that of a competitor. Thus, a dedication to continuous improvement must be guided by a *theory*.

The second layer of our theory points to three main drivers of success and sustainability that make for a fit between an organization's environment and its competitive advantage: environmental resources and capabilities and corresponding linkages. If implementation alone does not bring about a unique internal and external coalignment of resources and capabilities, then a continuous improvement program is simply costly and time-consuming.

In this chapter we will develop a third layer of our theory of continuous improvement and discuss the unique functions and conditions determining its effectiveness. In so doing we will (1) explain the importance of professional, technical, and practical knowledge as a basis for the third layer of our theory; (2) briefly discuss the need for continuous adaptation; (3) demonstrate the mixed record of continuous improvement efforts; (4) identify major questions answered by the theory of continuous improvement; (5) explore and analyze five major functions of continuous improvement; (6) investigate patterns and examples of three common types of improvement programs, namely, quality circles, total quality management, and work-outs.

THE FOUNDATION OF THE THEORY OF CONTINUOUS IMPROVEMENT

We concluded the previous chapter with a description of the three main sources of knowledge for organizations: professional, technical, and practical. Now we must relate these three types of knowledge to the continuous improvement process in order to explain why they are the foundation of our theory.

Professional knowledge resulting from general education is based upon philosophical principles and assumptions. It produces general theories, usually formed from a set of precise and integrated propositions that describe, explain, and predict certain phenomena. In effect, these theories verify either the basic principles of professional knowledge or their implications. Typical examples of such scientific theories are theories of relativity or gravity in physics, cognitive dissonance in psychology, and decision theory in management. Management theories based upon professional knowledge offer general guidelines on how to organize, make decisions, and motivate employees.

Technical knowledge is anchored in the description and explanation of processes. Therefore, in organizational settings, technical knowledge produces theories different from those produced by general knowledge. Theories based upon technical knowledge focus on empirical verification of relations that occur during the quantitative processes. Thus, a technically based theory, such as that explaining the complexity of the chemical process (the sequence and speed of reactions, implications of changing quantities of chemical compounds, and so forth), could lead to further analysis and development. Technical knowledge primarily offers facts to the continuous improvement process about the state of organizational processes, which allows for problem formulation. It offers technical and managerial solutions based upon the empirical explanation of specific inter- and intra-organizational relations.

Practical knowledge leads to empirically verifiable, local theories about how to perform managerial and other tasks. It therefore concentrates on the analysis of specific organizational processes and their effect (for example, how and when teamwork leads to improved quality, lower costs, and better productivity, as well as how to benchmark an unusually productive business process employed by a competitor). The core of the continuous improvement process is developed from practical knowledge as theories relate directly to the problems of organizational efficiency, effectiveness and competitive advantage.

Figure 2.1. graphically illustrates the impact of professional, technical, and practical knowledge on the continuous improvement process. It also illustrates one of the core problems with its application. While professional and technical knowledge build a body of public knowledge, the practical knowledge that is an essential part of the continuous improvement theory is partially tacit, and therefore difficult to unravel and analyze. In this way, a continuous improvement theory is a harmonious blend of general assumptions and principles, hard frameworks offered by technical knowledge and practical applications resulting from action research, consulting interventions, and case study analysis.

THE PURPOSE OF CONTINUOUS IMPROVEMENT

Organizational theory postulates and empirical research confirms that the performance impact of environment-organization

Figure 2.1

Professional, Technical, and Practical Knowledge as Sources of a Continuous-Improvement Theory

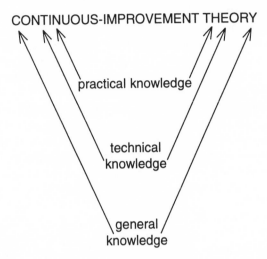

coalignment is simple and powerful. Successful organizations adapt to their environmental contingencies, while unsuccessful organizations fail to adjust to external conditions (Burns and Stalker 1961; Lawrence and Lorsch 1967; Venkatraman and Prescott 1990).

When the market is relatively stable, both in terms of consumer needs and companies' strategic behavior, the adaptation can occur slowly, by applying standard rules or developing new solutions through a process of trial and error. Stalk, Evans, and Shulman (1992: 62) describe this point:

> In a world characterized by durable products, stable customers needs, well-defined national and regional markets, and clearly identified competitors, competition was a "war of position" in which companies occupied competitive space like squares on a chessboard, building and defending markets share in clearly defined product or market segments. The key to competitive advantage was *where* a company chose to compete. *How* it chose to compete was also important but secondary, a matter of execution.

This traditional approach to competition has become obsolete for most companies due to the changes outlined in the previous chapter. Products life cycles have shrunk, markets are quickly saturated, consumers' needs and tastes are changing rapidly, and traditional market segmentation has broken down. The growing complexity, hostility, and speed of reaction has changed the nature of international competition. The dynamic interplay of environmental factor creates a constant need to revise the sources of a company's competitive advantage and increases the importance of adaptation.

The process of adaptation must be increasingly dynamic in order to ensure that a competitive advantage is attained and retained over time through proper internal and external coalignment, while ensuring that organizational flexibility does not suffer. As an example, consider the case of Emerson Electric, a successful, multi-business global competitor.

Emerson Electric

Emerson Electric is one of the America's leading manufacturers. In 1991 it celebrated its thirty-fourth consecutive year of improved earnings, higher earnings per share, and increased dividends. Such a performance record is difficult to match. At Emerson Electric, the bases of the adaptation process are similar to those at GE, in terms of perspective taken and outcome sought. Once a year, selected corporate officers meet with the management of each division for a confrontational planning conference. The managers describe the most important factors and trends in their respective markets and present plans of action. Each presentation is accompanied by four obligatory analyses, as illustrated in the following types of charts:

Value Measurement Chart. This illustration captures on one page all major financial trends, (for example, working capital, capital investment, return on capital, and sales) during the last five years along with projections for the next five years.

Sales Gap Chart. Current domestic and international sales are shown with the sources and level of growth for the next five years.

Sales Gap Line Chart. The division's development in terms of market penetration, price changes, new products, product line extensions, and international growth are shown.

5-back-by-forward P&L. This chart arranges detailed financial information from the current year as a threshold between the performance over the last five years and forecasted performance for the next five years in order to identify the trends and dicontinuities.

The company's CEO, Charles F. Knight (1992: 62) comments: "Together, these four charts tell us basic information about the business, alert us to any problems, and provide clues to the steps divisions must take to outperform the competition and produce results for stockholders...We want to hear division management's views of customers and markets; its plans for new products; its analysis of competition; and the status of such manufacturing issues as quality, capacity, productivity, inventory level, and compensation."

Knight clearly highlights the fundamental goal of continuous improvement: dynamic adaptation leading to company success. While the goal seems obvious, research shows that implementation of continuous improvement eludes most of U.S. and European organizations.

UNSUCCESSFUL ATTEMPTS AT
CONTINUOUS IMPROVEMENT

Florida Power & Light

In the late 1980s, Florida Power & Light, an American electrical utility, started one of the most comprehensive TQM programs in the United States. Almost three quarters of its intensively cross-trained employees were organized into 1,900 quality teams. The Quality Department used eighty-five employees to control a rigorous statistical quality review system. FP&L won the prestigious Japanese Deming Award in 1989 for outstanding quality achievements. Immediately after receiving the award, the company started to downsize the program. Improvements in the quality of services and benefits were insignificant compared with corresponding effort and costs. Formal methods and techniques dominated while the program lost content. The Quality Department was spun off into Qualtec, a quality consulting firm.

Wallace Company

Wallace Company, a U.S. distributor of pipe, valves and fittings for the oil, chemical, and petrochemical industries, embarked in 1989 upon an all-encompassing quality-improvement program based upon Deming Statistical Process Controls. The top management developed strategic objectives, later refined by the quality task force. More than one hundred task force groups and self-managed teams were established to guide and control the quality-improvement program. Using Statistical Process Controls, the company reviewed and restructured main processes and established quality-oriented links with suppliers. The company decided to push responsibility down the line, empowered its employees (for example, all associates were allowed to make customer-related decisions of up to $1000 without seeking approval), and decided to evaluate them on the base of their skills and ability to perform. In the Fall of 1990, Wallace Company received the Malcolm Baldrige National Quality Award.

The company ran into serious financial problems in 1991, which forced it to scale down the program, hire a turnaround specialist and lay off employees. In an analysis of the program and interview with Wallace's CEO and turnaround specialist, Hill and Freedman (1992) report that pursuit of quality in the case of Wallace Co. was a double-edged sword. On one side, the quality improved; however, the program proved to be too costly both in terms of expenditures and the opportunity costs of time expended by management.

Survey of Supporting Examples

Cases like these are abundant: Alcoa Corporation scrapped its decade-long continuous improvement program; the quality programs at British Telecom and Jaguar became bogged down by bureaucracy. Saab closed its new plant "of the future" in 1992 in which technology had been subordinated to the focus on teamwork and quality circles. Volvo's total quality program in the famous Kalmar factory in Sweden failed to produce a higher level of efficiency than that achieved by its competitors.

These cases cannot be dismissed with the argument that success depends solely upon implementation and situational conditions. Major studies show the same trend of failure in implementing continuous improvement programs as that illustrated by individual cases. Let us briefly review results of the most recent studies.

The Economist, a respected international economic magazine, discussed the results of two major recent studies in an article entitled, "The Cracks in Quality" (April 18th, 1992: 67–68). The first study, by A. T. Cracks, of over one hundred British firms, indicated that only a fifth of surveyed executives believed that their quality programs produced any "tangible results." The second survey, by Arthur D. Little, of 500 American manufacturing and service companies, found that executives in only one-third of the companies surveyed felt that their total quality programs were having "significant impact" on their competitiveness. Other surveys have drawn similar conclusions.

A McKinsey study of thirty quality programs found that two-thirds of them had either stalled or had not produced any real improvements (Fuchsbert 1992). In 1991, the American Electronics Association sponsored a survey of more than 300 electronics firms. The results reported by Schaffer and Thompson (1992) are shocking. While 73% of the companies implemented total quality programs, 63% had failed to improve quality defects by even 10%.

Perhaps the most comprehensive international study was undertaken in 1992 by Ernst and Young and the American Quality Foundation (Fuchsberg 1992). The study reports an increase in quality-related activities during 1989–1992 and details shortcomings across different quality improvement programs in 584 companies in the United States, Japan, Germany and Canada, in the auto, computer, banking, and health-care industries. Among the major findings of the study are the following observations:

1. Many companies isolate quality programs from day-to-day operations and thus do not achieve significant improvements.

2. Employee involvement in the programs is limited (for example, American computer companies involve just 12% of their employees, while automakers include only 28%; in the case of Canadian banks the proportion is 34%, and among Japanese carmakers, 78%).

3. Customer complaints are considered of "major or primary" importance as a source of information by only a limited number of companies (for example, for 73% of surveyed computer makers in Japan, 60% in Germany and only 26% in the United States).

4. Quality-performance measures (for example, defect rates, customer-satisfaction indices) were significantly less important than profitability and individual performance, especially in the United States.

These weak results of continuous improvement programs strongly suggest that we are in need of a theoretic framework that can guide successful implementations. We shall therefore (a) review theoretical functions to guide and focus the continuous improvement process; (b) apply these principles to analyze different types of improvement programs; and (c) evaluate the reasons for both success and failure.

THE THEORY OF CONTINUOUS IMPROVEMENT

The theory of continuous improvement is primarily drawn from practical knowledge that enables managers to analyze their environment and the firm's value chain. As we have already discussed, the analysis of a firm's environment should focus on the unique dynamic created by customer behavior and competitors' strategies. A value chain analysis should enable a firm to pinpoint its unique strengths and competencies residing in either specific functions, business processes, or linkages. Therefore the theoretical framework is established by answering the following key questions:

• Which products and product attributes do customers seek?

• Which strategies do competitors pursue? Do they develop products that combine multiple desirable attributes?

• Which core competencies enable an organization to provide the desirable product attributes better than its competitors?

- Which areas must a firm improve to develop or sustain a competitive advantage to provide products and cope with competition?
- Which tools and applications should be covered by a continuous improvement program?

THE FUNCTIONS OF CONTINUOUS IMPROVEMENT

The main goal and bottom line of the continuous improvement process is successful adaptation to environmental factors. Two major issues must be considered: the type of environment and competitive advantage. In order to learn why organizations are able to achieve an advantage in a given environment, we have utilized a systems approach. This approach explains how functional, business processes and environmental perspectives of an organization point to crucial factors of success. These factors include resources, capabilities, and linkages. However, we must now turn to *how* these factors are created and developed in practice.

There are five linked functions forming the basis of a successful continuous improvement program: (a) self-managed teams to improve the functioning of work units; (b) process mapping and improvement done by cross-functional teams; (c) benchmarking for reproduction of best practices; (d) strategic linkages for internal and external coalignment; and (e) creative breakthroughs for frame-breaking renewals.

These five functions build upon each other and create the final element of a comprehensive theory of continuous improvement as illustrated in Figure 2.2. Note that the theory addresses all three major challenges discussed in Chapter 1: (1) attainment of competitive advantage; (2) development of tacit, company-specific knowledge to improve and sustain market position; and (3) constant adaptation and innovation.

We separated the breakthrough function from the other four for two main reasons. First, coalignment, benchmarking, and cross-functional and self-managed teams operate within a framework created by previously developed linkages, resources and capabilities. The essence of breakthroughs lies in the fact that they aim at breaking that framework. While all functions have a dynamic component, the dynamism of the breakthrough function has a different logic than that of other four functions: it changes the actual setting in which an organization operates. Second, coalignment, benchmarking, and cross-functional and self-managed teams represent ongoing efforts to improve an organization, that is, to increase its competitive advantage in a given environment. Breakthroughs interrupt this trend of adaptation and start a new trend by either changing an organization's environment, its competitive advantage or both. Let us briefly review these five functions, as the following five chapters will expand on them in greater detail.

Self-Managed Teams: Problem Mapping

Self-managed teams are the building block of every continuous improvement program. They are vital as a tool for effective problem mapping. *Problem mapping is a team activity oriented toward locating, defining and solving problems in the workplace.* The use of self-managed teams as a tool for locating, defining, and solving problems in work settings, while standard in Japan, is only recently gaining popularity in Europe and the United States. In spite of many success stories recording the successful use of teamwork in companies, it is still difficult to evaluate the actual incorporation of self-managed teams as different surveys show conflicting results. However, the trend indicated by empirical research is evident.

A survey of 476 Fortune 1,000 companies, performed in 1990, showed that while only about 7% of the work force was organized into self-managed teams, half of the companies surveyed said that they would rely on teams in the future (Dumaine 1990). A 1991 nationwide survey conducted by Development Dimensions International, the Association for Quality and Participation, and Industry Week, revealed growing recognition of the importance of teams. Approximately 26% of the 862 executives surveyed was using teams in their organizations; others predicted a rapid increase in the use of team organization in the future (Wellings and George 1991).

Self-managed teams appear in many forms and under various names, for example, quality circles in Japan, self-managed or self-directed teams in the United States, and autonomous groups in Europe (Barry 1991; Magjuka 1991/92),

Figure 2.2

Theory of the Continuous-Improvement Process

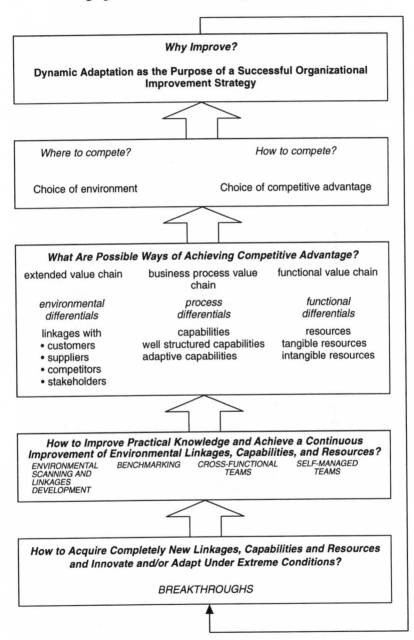

Why Improve?

Dynamic Adaptation as the Purpose of a Successful Organizational Improvement Strategy

Where to compete?   *How to compete?*

Choice of environment   Choice of competitive advantage

What Are Possible Ways of Achieving Competitive Advantage?

extended value chain	business process value chain	functional value chain
environmental differentials	*process differentials*	*functional differentials*
linkages with • customers • suppliers • competitors • stakeholders	capabilities well structured capabilities adaptive capabilities	resources tangible resources intangible resources

How to Improve Practical Knowledge and Achieve a Continuous Improvement of Environmental Linkages, Capabilities, and Resources?

ENVIRONMENTAL SCANNING AND LINKAGES DEVELOPMENT	*BENCHMARKING*	*CROSS-FUNCTIONAL TEAMS*	*SELF-MANAGED TEAMS*

How to Acquire Completely New Linkages, Capabilities and Resources and Innovate and/or Adapt Under Extreme Conditions?

BREAKTHROUGHS

but all exhibit common features. The three most crucial commonalities are homogeneity, cross training, and empowerment. Let us outline each of these factors:

Homogeneity.   Self-managed teams are groups developed from work units. As a result, self-managed teams are relatively homogenous in terms of work environment and members' tasks (for example, maintenance unit, assembly line workers, purchasing department). The common tasks and work environment encourage the granting of well-defined power and responsibility to solve problems connected with the execution of common tasks.

Cross Training.   Self-managed teams develop their members' knowledge base, experience, and skills through cross-training and common problem solving. This practice helps to expand employees' knowledge base and motivational level (Krafcik 1989). All members become capable of playing diverse roles, understanding the unit's purpose, function, and relations with other units, and formulating and solving problems.

Empowerment.   Teamwork must be structured to encourage problem solving and an orientation toward process improvement. A necessary condition to effect these goals is empowerment of the teams. Empowerment should be focused in certain areas, clearly related to problem mapping and the problem-solving process. Only then are decisions and resources moved closer to where action can be taken, as Benson (1992: 30) succinctly states: "In most such cases, the employees who work within the processes every day understand the problems more intimately than anyone else. They are the ones, after all, who jump through often ridiculous hoops to get their jobs done. And usually, they're the ones who remember why the hoops were invented in the first place."

In summarizing our description of self-managed teams operating in the workplace, we can see that they are effective if tasks are well-defined, members are cross-trained, and teams are empowered with decision-making competencies that enable them to not only remove evident deficiencies but effect improvements.

Self-managed teams are a natural and necessary extension of process-oriented, cross-functional teams. While self-managed teams look for improvements in their limited natural workspace, cross-functional teams link multiple workspaces and prevent the incorporation of local improvements to the detriment of the organization's operations as a whole.

Cross-Functional Teams: Mapping Processes

The strategic perspective of an organization as a system, which was presented in Chapter 1, stresses two features. First, it stresses that an organization should be viewed as a value chain of systemically inter-related functions and processes concerning product/service development, manufacturing, customer service and management. A map of these processes is the key to truly understanding how they are interrelated, and how complex manufacturing, finance, and other operations are accomplished. Second, mapping points to the need to extend organizational analysis into the environment and build maps of an organization's potential linkages with competitors, consumers, suppliers. The most effective way to build reliable maps is by applying cross-functional teams.

Cross-functional teams have a long history in organizational practice. When a cross-functional team was used to solve particular complex problems, it was called a "task force." During the seventies and eighties they became more permanent structural elements with the development of matrix structures. Now they are gaining recognition as tools of process mapping. *Process mapping refers to the elaborate and systemic effort of cross-functional teams to develop models (usually in the form of flow charts) of organizational processes for the purpose of reengineering and simplification.*

Three common features of organizational processes put cross-functional teams in the best position to map processes. Organizational processes are repetitive and cross-functional, and demand extensive coordination of knowledge and activities. Let us review these characteristics.

Repetitive. Most processes are repetitive because they constitute standardized activities with the same inputs and outputs, for example, billing customers, maintaining machinery and equipment, and planning and executing production. The repetitive nature of the processes makes them relatively easy to monitor, record, analyze, and subsequently improve.

Cross-functional. Organizational processes encompass and cross multiple functions. Knowledge of the relevant functions is necessary for effective analysis. In practice, organizational processes are often much more complex than necessary. Each of the top or middle managers see only part of the process and thus modify it over time according to the interests and/or needs of his or her subsystem, without regard for the efficiency of the process as a whole. Such changes and "improvements" lead to growing complexity and major problems at the cross-functional points. These problems are often overlooked simply because they are not within any one person's functional responsibility. R. Walker (1992: 16) makes the following observations based on his experiences at Xerox Corporation:

> When we then overlaid this process view of our business with our functional organization we made some very interesting observations. First, *just about every process was cross functional,* in that more than one function participated in delivering parts of the process...The second observation was the most telling. When we then analyzed the process for efficiency and effectiveness we found 80.9% percent of errors, queuing, duplication of activity were at the functional cross-over points.

Coordination. Most organizational processes have a double-helix structure, that is, they consist of flows of material components (parts, people), and flows of coded information. Such patterns of organizational processed demand superior coordination of materials and information flows. However, the design of material flows is basically production-based, that is, dominated by primary functions, while the design of information flows results primarily from the needs of management, and is thereby dominated by support functions. The different functional bases of design often result in a lack of coordination between the tangible (production) and intangible (informational) aspects of any process. Cross-functional teams help both to simplify and integrate these processes.

Benchmarking: Reproduction of Best Practices

The excellent management practices that result in customer satisfaction can be developed in two ways: managers either develop them in-house or copy them. The first method, though costly and time-consuming, has dominated for decades as a trial-and-error evolutionary process. The second way, called benchmarking, has only recently become widely accepted as a viable option. *The essence of benchmarking is to seek out, learn, and implement the best practices of top market performers (both competitors and non-competitors).* Benchmarking supplements negotiated linkages, in that it forces companies to focus on the marketplace and appreciate that there exist organizations which can serve as role models and customers with changing needs.

One of the first documented attempts to map best practices was made by Xerox in 1980–1981, when the company discovered that its market was invaded by strong Japanese competitors. Rob Walker (1992: 9), Director of Business Management Systems and Quality at Rank Xerox (UK), explains:

> The first action we took was to institute a process we call "competitive benchmarking"...We looked at how competition developed a product, how much it cost them to make it, how they distributed it, how they marketed and sold it, how they billed it, how they supported it, how their organization worked and what technology supported them. The results were shocking. One study found that Xerox's unit manufacturing cost was equal to the Japanese U.S. selling price—and they were making a profit...It took us twice as long as the Japanese to bring a new product to market. We used five times the number of engineers, had four times the number of design changes and three times the design costs. We had over 30,000 defective parts per million compared to their less than 1000 defective parts per million.

The company decided to map in detail the best practices used by competitors and implemented them (sometimes in innovative ways) to improve over sixty key work processes that had been identified as problematic. Over time Xerox revised its system and extended its approach to benchmarking to search for best practices and clues in three ways.

Outside Industry. The company started to search for best practices outside its industry, benchmarking American Express for billing and collections, American Hospital Supply for automated inventory control, and L.L. Bean for distribution, warehousing, and order-taking.

Inside Industry. Xerox began to use extensive customer surveys to benchmark for customer satisfaction and compare itself against the competition in such key areas as sales responsiveness and product performance.

Inside Company. Xerox started to search for best practices internally, supporting the diffusion of the best solutions across its international operations.

The major advantages of benchmarking as a part of systematic improvement process are threefold (Altany 1991). First,
benchmarking considerably speeds up the improvement process
by allowing the identification of relatively inefficient operations
and quickly incorporating existing solutions. Second, benchmarking expands the improvement focus by allowing the consideration of possible improvements along all functions, processes,
and linkages, instead of improvement of only the most visible
and easily analyzed end-products and services on which companies typically concentrate. In effect, a company can benchmark
processes along specific primary and support activities, but also
along such complex processes as leadership or linkages with
suppliers or customers. Finally, benchmarking speeds up the
implementation process because it leads to the introduction of
solutions that have been tested and experienced (through data
collection and analysis) by managers of the company pursuing
the improvement practice. D. Altany (1991: 17) concludes:

> This focus on continuous improvement and the pursuit
> of excellence is the feature that gives benchmarking
> such power when put into practice. Although at first
> glance benchmarking may appear to be geared toward
> one-time gains, the opposite is really true. By formal-
> izing and institutionalizing the process by which compa-
> nies ferret out and incorporate leading-edge business
> practices, benchmarking helps to create a corporate
> culture that encourages the pursuit of innovations—
> both from within and outside the company.

Developing Strategic Linkages

Any organization that performs in a turbulent environment
has to analyze its environment and develop strategic linkages.
The importance of linkages is clearly explained by K. Ohmae
(1989): "You can do everything yourself—with enough time,
money and luck. But all three are in short supply....Global-
ization mandates alliances, makes them absolutely essential to
strategy."

*Strategic linkages can be defined as a set of internal and
external linkages that are critically important for an organization's coalignment with its environment and thus for its sustain-*

able competitive advantage. The process of developing linkages consists of three major steps:

- systematic environmental scanning for an understanding of the general environment
- map of potential partners in terms of interests, concerns and potential contributions to coalignment
- development of short- and long-term strategic linkages to enhance an organization's ability to adapt and compete

The outcomes of each step are inputs for the next. While there are different ways to describe an environment relevant to an organization, a useful starting point was offered by Hall (1982) with his identification of two types of organizational environment: close and distant. A distant environment consists of those elements that cannot be influenced by an organization's actions but still regulates or influences them. A close environment consists of those elements that both influence organizational performance and can be in turn influenced by managers. In following this distinction, an environmental analysis would map two sets of forces. In analyzing the distant environment, general data is gathered and analyzed concerning social, economic, technological, and legal trends and activities. Both direct and indirect impacts on organizational performance should be considered. A detailed analysis of the close environment looks at relevant threats and opportunities in order to focus on the key strategic issues for the particular company. Threats are those trends or events that may diminish company performance; opportunities may be used to enhance it. Such an analysis should enable a company to build a model of its environment and to identify defining characteristics such as industrial boundaries, structure, maturity, exposure to international competition, and propensity of technological and managerial breakthroughs, and thereby to select an appropriate strategy.

The next step is adding the major stakeholders to the environmental map: suppliers, customers, and competitors, together with their existing linkages. A map of existing and potential linkage partners allows for an analysis of the interests, concerns, and possible contributions of potential partners, as well as of the strengths and weaknesses of existing linkages.

The third step involves a choice of linkages in terms of partners, types, and strengths. Illustrating these strategic choices,

Nohria and Garcia-Pont (1991) performed a powerful analysis of strategic linkages among 35 major global automobile producers during 1980–1990. Using sophisticated statistical apparatus, the authors showed that the industry was divided into eleven strategic groups as defined as firms with similar strategic capabilities.[4] The authors then hypothesized that the network of linkages in an industry is not randomly patterned but is structured as strategic blocs of two main types: a complementary bloc of firms from different strategic groups with complementary capabilities, and a pooling bloc composed of firms from the same strategic group pooling their resources. The results of the analysis confirmed the authors' hypothesis. Six strategic blocs, representing a continuum of complementary pooling blocs, were identified. The exemplary pooling bloc consisted of a set of European firms: Fiat (including Ferrari and Alfa Romeo acquired by Fiat), PSA, Renault and Volvo. These firms established a dense set of linkages for cooperative component manufacture and technology development. The exemplary complementary bloc consisted of six firms belonging to different strategic groups: Ford, Jaguar, KIA, Lio Ho, Mazda, and Nissan. The bloc was centered around Ford with a set of technology development, manufacturing, and marketing agreements. The net effect of the blocs' existence is paradoxical. The blocs become similar in terms of their strategic capabilities;[5] hence, capabilities in each bloc become similar over time.

Three major advantages offered by linkages (Ohmae 1989; Nohria and Garcia-Pont 1991) include (1) stabilizing the environment by establishing coordinated and negotiated patterns of action, shaping competition, and reducing uncertainty about stakeholders' interests and concerns; (2) allowing firms to gain fast access to desired resources and knowledge-based expertise to enhance performance and facilitate learning; and (3) supplementing internally-based improvement in the short-term and increasing its potential in the long run.

BREAKTHROUGHS: FUTURE MAPPING

When the competitive advantage gained from new management practices lessens, because of their increasingly universal application, a few firms seeking new competitive advantage

begin charting the course to yet another business-wide transition or management era. Eventually, successive business-wide transition and management eras begin producing only marginal advantages and benefits, thus setting the stage for a fundamental shift or transformation.
Hickman and Silva (1987: 8)

The four functions we have discussed thus far, namely, mapping the environment, best-practices, processes and problems have only a limited time dimension. They are relatively incremental and linear. The incremental nature of these functions results from the assumption that the trends and patterns both in the environment and within the organization will, more or less, continue. Their linearity stems from the functions' orientation towards improvements within the frame of the existing situation, within known opportunities, threats, limitations, and possibilities. Thus, they operate mainly in the problem-solution loop, where new problems arise or solutions become obsolete.

Future mapping operates in the opportunity-possibility loop and lets one search for possible discontinuities and for frame-breaking developments that might occur naturally or be effected either in the organization or in its environment. These discontinuities can either be an event that an organization can quickly develop, such as with Sony's exploitation of the transistor, or a major crisis that changes the structure of the industry or general environment, such as with the oil crisis. In either case environmental changes force an organization to respond with a breakthrough strategy to establish a revised foundation for future developments.

The two major types of breakthroughs are focused and diffused. A focused breakthrough is a frame-breaking change within an organizational line or staff function of the value chain. In contrast, a diffused breakthrough occurs at the process or linkage level.

Focused Breakthrough.   The most typical focused breakthroughs occur in the area of research and development and lead to new technologies and/or products. Technological break-throughs such as the development of the transistor and later the large-scale integration circuits enabled the development of personal computers and laptops. However, focused break-through can also occur in other functions, such as procurement, operations, or marketing. The battle of two ulcer drugs, Zantac and Tagamet, illustrates a marketing breakthrough.

Soon after SmithKline began marketing Tagamet, an anti-ulcer drug, in 1977, it became a market success. However, SmithKline relied on its own limited sales force and did not invest in marketing. Glaxo developed a similar anti-ulcer drug, Zantac, in 1981. Despite a U.S. price 50% higher than that of Tagamet, sales of Zantac quickly surpassed those of SmithKline's product. The Glaxo breakthrough occurred in marketing. Rather than limiting sales efforts to its own sales force, Glaxo contracted the Hoffmann-La Roche army of salespeople to promote Zantac around the world and invested heavily in advertising. This marketing strategy (now copied by other drug companies) resulted in 1992 U.S. sales of $1.73 billion as compared with Tagamet's $647 million.

Diffused Breakthrough. A diffused breakthrough changes the design and linkages of the processes across an organization. Such a breakthrough results in a unique configuration of the company's processes and linkages, thus creating an opportunity for a new competitive advantage, as shown by Toyota's lean production system. The company successfully enriched and expanded workers' jobs by staffing assembly lines with teams of cross-trained workers. Small autonomous work teams proved capable of work standardization, quality improvement and quick adaptation to the shirts and changes in production. A just-in-time delivery system reduced the direct and indirect costs of production and tied suppliers more closely to the company. Close cooperation among the research, market testing, product design, production, and manufacturing functions decreased development time for new car models (Sasaki 1991; Womack, Jones, and Roos 1990).

None of the tools, techniques or methods of production used by Toyota is unknown or difficult to imitate, whereas a system of production created to link these elements and develop a high-speed process is a breakthrough in the concept of production, as suggested by Cusumano (1988: 38):

There was nothing mysterious or miraculous about what Toyota and other Japanese automakers accomplished in manufacturing. They responded to specific market conditions, creatively applying techniques first developed in the U.S. in new ways. Ultimately, by seeking a better solution to a fundamental problem, the Japanese set new standards of efficiency and started a revolution in manufacturing theory and practice that has yet to end.

Breakthroughs are a necessary element of the continuous improvement movement. They are punctuations, often not fully developed or operational at the time of inception, that can be improved over time until the marginal costs of improvement exceed the benefits. As long as they are not patented, breakthroughs are a worthwhile target for benchmarking. General Motors developed a multidivisional structure in the 1920s to monitor and control production and sales in separate market segments; eventually this structure became a model of organizational design worldwide. In the 1930s, Sears adopted a matrix structure. It combined the territorial structure of five geographical areas comprised of thirty-three districts with the functional management of merchandising, operations, accounting, and finance. This organizational breakthrough was so difficult to copy and master that the matrix structure was widely adopted and improved by business organizations only years later, in the 1960s and 1970s.

Philips' development of the video-recorder is an example of a technological breakthrough. However, Japanese companies improved the product and its technology to such an extent that it became a commercial breakthrough. Thus, even continuous improvement models experience breakthroughs. Quality circles were the first systematic type of continuous improvement. Later, the total quality management approach was a further breakthrough due to its systemization and breadth. Work-Out, developed by General Electric, is a new type of continuous improvement model consisting of a systemic combination of previously developed methods. We will discuss these three types of continuous improvement programs as standard models in this field.

THREE TYPES OF CONTINUOUS IMPROVEMENT PROGRAM

The tradition of CIP is not new; Schroeder and Robinson (1991) provide a thorough discussion of some early systems developed in the nineteenth century by Denny of Dumbarton, a Scottish shipbuilder; and John H. Patterson at National Cash Register; as well as a comprehensive system developed at the beginning of the century by the Lincoln Electric Company. While individual CIPs existed and shared some common features such as suggestion boxes, quality and quantity based wages, and training, they were still relatively rare and unique to the companies that developed and applied them. The programs that became in recent years standard models of CIP are quality circles (QC), total quality management (TQM), and innovative Work-Out as developed by General Electric.

Quality Circles

Quality circles[7] are based on the premise that improvement must stem from the collective intelligence of the whole organization and that people who perform a task are the prime source of suggestions on how it can be improved. QCs spread across Japan in the fifties and sixties as a result of "push and pull" forces to improve quality. The Ministry of International Trade and Industry (MITI) encouraged the adoption of the demanding Japanese Industrial Standards, while various awards for superior quality, the best known being the Deming Prize and All-Japan Quality Award, were established (see Watanabe 1991).

The most simple definition of the quality circle is that it is *a group of employees that meets regularly to solve problems affecting its work area* (Adam 1991). Most of the leading Japanese firms rely heavily on these voluntary groupings of six to twelve workers to generate suggestions for improvement and attribute them for quality improvements. QCs also became popular in the 1980s in Europe and the United States where increasing numbers of large and middle-sized companies adopted QC programs (Lawler and Mohram 1985; Dulworth, Landen, and Usilaner 1990). Quality circles usually perform in the following way (see Garvin 1984):

- Group formation. The workers decide on a voluntary basis to create a quality circle in their work area. Managers cannot force workers to form QCs, but may skillfully use peer pressure and rewards to encourage workers.

- Analytical skill development. The workers are trained in basic statistical methods and problem-solving skills; they can also call on experts from other departments to assist them in data gathering and analysis.

- Targets established. QCs establish quantitative targets for quality improvement on the basis of their expertise in the particular work area, as well as information on defects and problems collected, compiled, and analyzed for trends by the firm's specialized departments.

- Suggestion formation. Participants decide on the problem or potential improvement area, collect and analyze data, formulate and evaluate solutions, and pass their suggestions along to their managers. The whole process of problem solving is coordinated and facilitated by a quality circle leader.

- Suggestions reviewed. The proposed solutions are reviewed by supervisors and/or committees and approved for implementation.

The concept of quality circles has some major strengths. First, it recognized the necessity of involving organizational members in the improvement process. Second, the voluntary participation and on-going training and education program instituted by the QC concept enables quality circles to perform as an effective self-managed team. Third, quality circles are multi-functional. While the major role of QCs is that of problem solving role, they also allow for coordination, integration, and maintenance of the organization's social fabric.

In spite of these strengths, quality circles introduced in United States' and European organizations often fail. Two specific reasons most frequently cited for this failure are a lack of integration of QCs with mainstream operating processes and the waning commitment of managers bored or dissatisfied with the concept (Dulworth et al. 1990). However, quality circles also have limitations as a type of continuous improvement program. They do not include the issues of the environment, best practices, and future mapping. Therefore, they may be part of an improvement program but cannot be the final solution in the typical business environment.

Total Quality Management

Total quality management developed from the work of four influential theorists: E. Demming's statistical process control approach, P. Crosby's zero-defects approach, J. M. Juran's total quality management, and A. V. Feigenbaum's total quality control perspectives (Kathawala 1989). Each of them had a different perspective and advocated slightly different approaches and techniques:[8] they all have had a lasting influence on the development of the total quality management concept. Each of the four theories was, over time, enriched, modified, and applied in different ways by various organizations making the whole concept of TQM elusive and eclectic. In order to present TQM in a more classic version we will present Demming's approach as it provides both a rationale and underlying philosophy (Walton 1986).

According to Demming (1982; 1986) improvements are not possible without statistical process control to exploit control charts, Pareto charts, histograms, scatter diagrams and other tools. However, tools are of secondary importance: management of quality is primary a way of thinking, a view towards examining processes from a long-term perspective and searching for underlaying causal relations and possible improvements. The TQM process consists of two stages, in both of which management plays a key role. In the first stage the company absorbs and implements several rules of behavior to facilitate the transformation from reactive to proactive and quality-oriented, as outlined below in Deming's fourteen points. In the second stage, organizational processes become a focus of constant improvement via the use of statistical tools. Let us briefly review these two stages, starting with Deming's essential postulates addressed to the new type of quality-driven organization:

1. Create constancy of purpose for the improvement of product and service in order to stay in business and be competitive.

2. New economic age demands new philosophy. Quality must become a "way of life" because customers do not stand for the past level of mistakes and defects.

3. Quality must be built into the process and product as quality cannot be achieved through mass inspection and control.

4. Minimize total costs and end the practice of awarding business on the basis of price tag. Strive for good relations with single suppliers based on trust and loyalty.

5. Strive for constant improvement of quality and productivity, as well as for reduction of costs.

6. Institute ongoing training on the job that enhances process improvements.

7. Institute leadership that facilitates workers and managers to do a better job by understanding tasks, placing employees in the "right" position, and identifying and eliminating barriers that hinder performance.

8. Empower the workforce, allow expression of new ideas and concerns, and drive out fear so everyone can work effectively.

9. Break down barriers between functional departments and use cross functional teams in order to ensure proper coordination and open communication.

10. Eliminate slogans and targets (like zero defects) promoting only frustration and resentment.

11. Eliminate standards (quotas) and management by objectives (numbers) that do not assist employees in improving the work process and substitute leadership instead.

12. Remove barriers that rob the hourly worker of his/her right to pride of workmanship; shift from stressing sheer numbers to quality.

13. Institute a vigorous program of education, training, and retraining.

14. Make the transformation of the organization everybody's responsibility and enforce active participation of employees in the quality oriented system.

The implementation of these fourteen points should, in Deming's view, enable an organization to create a climate and conditions for successful, systematized improvements of organizational processes. The five fundamental stages of Deming's (1986) Process Management are as follows:

1. *Define the process:* Document the current process through flow-charting, identification of inputs and outputs and key quality characteristics.

2. *Make obvious improvements:* Simplify the process and eliminate redundant steps, slack, and waste as allowed through inexpensive, easily evaluated and easily implemented improvements.

3. *Apply statistical control to the process:* Statistical controls are useful for understanding common cause variation (always present in the process) and special cause variation (occasionally present variation that should be eliminated).

4. *Utilize information:* Improve the process for incorporating information gained through statistical process control in order to develop incremental changes.

5. *Monitor and control:* Monitor and adjust the process as necessary.

Total quality management is a much more complex and far-reaching approach than that employed by quality circles due to its attention to adaptation, coordination, and empowerment.

Adaptation.   Deming's approach recognizes the importance of adaptation as a goal of continuous improvement, even if he concentrates primarily on quality driven advantages. The environmental demands brought on by competitors and customers are a major factor shaping TQM. However, Deming's theory does not formally address the importance of negotiated linkages and benchmarking, thus leaving the focus of the improvement program primarily inside the organization.

Coordination.   TQM recognizes the importance of integration and coordination among specialized subsystems. It stresses cross-functional orientation and teamwork, even while remaining rather vague in terms of practical implementation.

Empowerment.   Similar to QCs, Deming's approach emphasizes participation, empowerment, and skill development on the part of the participants. Patten (1991/1992: 10) explains: "The organization whose managers and employees are not empowered, energized, or enable to relate to one another and share their infinite resources must engage in a deep and extensive process of skill development before TQM can take hold."

While we agree in principle with the orientation, we do not accept Deming's notion that productivity targets and numerical goals encourage manipulation, thereby contributing to low morale and cooperation. One of the key success factors of continuous improvement programs is monitoring and control of results. The value of the program lies both in the results achieved and in the activities performed. Such an approach is visible in the Work-Out concept.

Work-Outs

Work-Outs were developed by General Electric in 1989 with the idea that continuous improvement must become second nature at GE to create a lean, mean, and boundaryless company (Tichy and Charzon 1989; Stewart 1991; Flynn and Care 1994; Cushman and King 1995). Work-Out is one of three parts of GE's continuous improvement program: the search for Best Practices, Process Mapping, and Work-Outs. It is essentially a problem-solving meeting of employees from varying ranks and job functions across the organization, with the potential participation of suppliers and/or customers. The meeting lasts from one to three days and includes 40 to 100 people. The meetings are structured in the following way:

- Opening. The manager (division or plant head) opens the meeting with a presentation of GE's values, the key market issues, and a competitor analysis. The organization's vision of matching GE's values with market demands, through continuous improvement by lower costs and increased quality and speed, is outlined. Then the manager sketches out a rough agenda of the Work-Out and leaves the meeting.

- Small groups. The group breaks into small teams led by trained facilitators. After some team building and integrating activities, members of the team concentrate on the analysis of problems and debate potential solutions.

- Presentation. The team prioritizes the solutions, builds cost/benefit analyses and action plans, and prepared the final presentation. The manager, unaware of what the groups have decided, then returns to listen to the presentations. In principle, the manager should either make immediate decisions on particular solutions and the team proposals, ask for more information, or at least deliver thorough evaluations of the proposals.

The design of the Work-Out is both common and innovative at the same time. It contains all classic organizational development techniques: cross-functional composition of members, problem-orientation, stages of integration and socialization, brainstorming, and delayed evaluation. The Work-Outs also follow a well-known precept: first they concentrate on minor but irritating issues, and thereby allow for the initial development of easier solutions to build trust and a cooperative attitude (Stewart 1991).

However, the innovative features of Work-Outs are particularly interesting. First, the meetings are well-structured and result-oriented, and conclude, according to the design, with manager's concrete decisions on implementation. Second, Work-outs include customers, suppliers and colleagues from other GE divisions, thus tapping the major source of complex problems: internal and external linkages. Such an innovative approach promises more permanent solutions to problems. Third, Work-Outs are employed on a mass-scale and have positive educational, training, and cultural side effects. Finally, from the beginning they served part of a larger design, as Work-Outs have become the key tool for spreading the two additional instruments of continuous improvement program throughout the organization. Work-Outs can be used as a springboard for benchmarking to identify the practices needing improvement and to direct the search for best solutions. Later, these meetings simplify and facilitate the analysis and sharing of Best Practices. Also, Work-Outs are ideal settings for the development of Process-Owners: teams whose responsibility and authority cross over departmental or divisional boundaries. Only such cross-functional teams can successfully build maps of the processes and look for improvements.

Key Success Factors

There are three key success factors of continuous improvement programs that are evident from both the successes and failures we have discussed and from the theory we have developed. These factors are 1) the integration with daily operations; 2) the alignment with the type of organizational environment; and 3) a dual focus on process and results. Let us review them briefly:

Integration with Daily Operations. Continuous improvement must be fully integrated into organizational operations to avoid becoming a set of side experiments. Without such integration, CIP will fail. First, all changes and improvements are initially costly, time-consuming and a cause of dislocation. It took Toyota more than twenty years to perfect its lean manufacturing operations as a harmonious system of machines, procedures, and employees. Shigeo Shingo (1987: 152), one of the leading Japanese experts, comments on Japanese experiences:

> Since improvements to a greater or lesser extent demand new procedures, a certain amount of difficulty will be encountered and a certain amount of time will be needed to decide how to carry out those procedures and then to memorize them. Initially, the new methods will be difficult...Thus, no improvement shows its true worth right away. Its real efficacy will become apparent only after a certain period of practice. This means that 99 percent of all improvement plans would vanish without a trace if they were to be abandoned after only a brief trial. People in charge of plan improvement must grasp this fact.

Second, continuous improvement's lack of integration with operations hampers the improvement of the crucial internal and external linkages, as improvements are directed toward easily identifiable problems confined to the work area.

Third, separation of continuous improvement from operations almost inevitable reduces the flow of ideas and involvement because companies and managers profit from productivity gains in primitive ways. As Schroeder and Robinson (1991) argue, the practice of rewarding such gains by cutting the workforce and reducing allocated resources is quite common. Thus the message is as clear as it is demoralizing: improvements may cost resources as well as jobs.

Alignment with an Organization's Environment. All improvements have their benefits and costs; however, the net effect depends upon the internal and external alignment. Strong empirical evidence supporting this relation was recently presented in an excellent study by Venkartaman and Prescott (1990), which we present in more detail in the chapter on linkages. For now, we will state that the study confirms that the direction of improvement advances can critically influence the effects. Misguided improvement efforts, those not applicable to the particular type of environment, might worsen instead of improve the company's position and performance. For example, for a company operating in a mature market, a continuous improvement program would yield the best results if concentrated on ways to lower investment intensity, direct costs, and marketing revenue, while increasing relative market share and tying compensation directly to performance. In new markets increases of employee productivity, product quality and lower marketing/revenue are major targets for improvement.

Process and Result Oriented. This issue is closely related to the alignment orientation just discussed. While continuous improvement is by definition a process, it must be clearly focused on results. Managing and improving processes through mapping the environment, best practices, problems, and processes are not worthwhile without visible, measurable results. Schaffer and Thompson (1992: 80) commented on this point: "The performance improvement efforts of many companies have as much impact on operational and financial results as a ceremonial rain dance has on the weather. While some companies constantly improve measurable performance, in many other, managers continue to dance round and round the campfire - exuding faith and dissipating energy."

Schaffer and Thompson (1992) offer four arguments as to why the clear focus on results is important. First, desired results focus attention and effort and are useful for prioritizing potential improvements. Second, as subsequent improvements are introduced and tied to results, the company can calibrate its approach to continuous improvement and adapt its general functions to suit particular internal and external contingencies. Third, in order to match the high-speed changes in the environment and maintain high levels of motivation and involvement, measurable results that are easy to grasp, understand, and promote should be fed back into the improvement process. Tangible results of the improvement program help build confidence and reinforce behavior on the part of the managers and employees. Without their support, the program risks mediocrity and superficial participation.

Finally, as each improvement project serves as a measurable testing ground, management can gradually accumulate knowledge and experience, compare Best Practices and results, and expand the program throughout the organization in a controlled fashion.

CONCLUSIONS

Building on the concepts presented in Chapter 1, namely, (1) relationships among strategy, environment and competitive advantage, and (2) resources, capabilities and linkages, this chapter began with the idea that demands for high-speed adaptation create a need for continuous improvement programs. We then explored answers to the question, "How can we build practical, tacit knowledge and achieve in practice a continuous improvement of environmental linkages, capabilities, and resources?" We developed five functions of continuous improvement, along with practical principles and methods for their implementation. We discussed how the environment, best practices, processes, and problems are mapped and addressed through linkages, benchmarking, self-managed and cross-functional teams, and breakthroughs. Then we applied this framework to a critical analysis of the main types of continuous improvement programs: quality circles, total quality management, and Work-Outs, pointing out their theoretical and practical strengths and weaknesses. This analysis led to the exploration of three key success factors for the application of continuous improvement.

Our goal throughout the chapter has been to derive a theory that can guide our understanding of effective continuous improvement processes. In order to make the theory more specific and useful for practical application, we shall now consider a detailed theoretical explanation and practical examples of each of the five main functions, and in the process of doing so link them into a coherent system.

THREE

Self-Managed Teams

Teamwork is an essential part of effective teams. You do not need a team to
have teamwork, but you do need
teamwork to have a team. (Denton,
1992: 87)

Two types of teams are basic building blocks of any continuous
improvement program: self-managed and cross-functional. In
the next two chapters we shall discuss the role, scope, and tools
of effective teamwork. The point of departure is a definition of
teamwork that outlines three defining attitudes and behaviors
that focus on goals, interests, and values. (Barrett 1987).

    Common Goal. Teams are effective only if they have a
common focus or goal. Each member of the team must participate in identifying the goal in order to share the commitment. It
is this collective effort of establishing and publicly committing to
a shared goal (in front of one's co-workers) which separates a
mere collection of individuals from an integrated team.

    Integration of Members' Interests. Team effort demands
that unique interests, concerns and contributions of each team
member are clearly articulated, understood and appropriately
integrated into the team's performance. Only then can team
members become committed to a common course of action,
focus their energy, and perform to high standards.

    Team Values. Effective teamwork demands that a culture
be built on values such as unconditional trust, confidence, and
mutual respect.

    All three features are closely interrelated in an effort to
develop jointly established and publicly supported goals and an

integrated team with its own culture. Combining individual members' unique interests, concerns, and contributions creates a team synergy and helps to sustain a common culture. Collaboration guided by trust and mutual respect produces a collective commitment and focuses each team member on the common goal. The presence of all three factors is necessary and collectively sufficient to produce a productive team. The purpose of this chapter is to operationalize this definition of teamwork in relation to self-managed teams. More specifically we shall (1) introduce the purpose, problem-solving techniques, and types of self-managed teams; (2) present the main tools used by effective self-managed teams; (3) discuss in detail the role, scope, and practical operations of different types of self-managed teams; and (4) examine the critical success factors of self-managed teams.

INTRODUCTION OF SELF-MANAGED TEAMS: THEIR PURPOSE, TECHNIQUES OF PROBLEM SOLVING, AND MAIN TYPES

A key purpose of self-managed teams is to personally involve employees in matters of company performance and product quality. A survey conducted by the American Association for Quality and Participation of 531 member companies identified the following purposes of self-managed teams:

- improving organizational communications
- improving productivity
- reducing costs
- improving product quality
- improving production or service dependability
- providing employees with a voice in company affairs
- satisfying employees' psychological needs
- improving process flexibility
- increasing organizational innovation

Surveyed enterprises utilized self-managed teams for an average of 4.2 years. Different objectives were behind the implementation of three types of self-managed teams, as identified by Magjuka (1991/1992: 52): production teams, quality circles, and problem solving teams.

- Production teams consist of groups of employees given substantial responsibility for the planning, organizing and scheduling of production processes. They are created mainly to improve product quality, increase process dependability, and reduce costs.

- Quality circles are groups of employees that meet to improve operations of their units. They are created to improve communication and product quality, and to provide employees with a voice in company affairs and a better opportunity to satisfy their needs.

- Problem-solving teams are often formed on an ad hoc basis to solve problems identified in the work units. They are focused on improved communication and employee performance. Employee involvement leads to greater job satisfaction and, consequently, to higher performance (Magjuka 1991/1992).

The common denominator of the purposes identified for employee teams is increased performance levels. A generic way to improve performance is to formulate and solve problems encountered in their work environment. Beginning in the 1950s, researchers attempted to define the common sequence of activities which led to effective problem solving. Following Dewey's reflecting thinking model, it was argued that effective team problem-solving has five stages:

1. locating and defining the problem
2. examining causes of the problem
3. exploring possible solutions
4. testing various solutions
5. selecting and implementing the best solution

In spite of the fact that different researchers selected slightly different terms to describe the stages of problem solving, their logic is similar. There is also a growing understanding and belief that these stages do not constitute a well-organized sequence. Teams often proceed in interactive loops, not in linear development stages, and the problem-solving process appears diverse, mediated by many specific and situational variables (Cushman and King 1995). The process, however, is regulated by the logic of tools applied by various teams. Let us now briefly review the most important problem-solving tools and then discuss, in detail, the operation of each type of self-managed team.

Tools for Effective Problem-Solving

While most of the tools used by self-managed teams are simple, application may be more complex. In order to success-fully formulate and solve organizational problems in their work environment, self-managed groups must be able to use several tools for problem formulation, data collection and analysis, and the evaluation of solutions. The following nine commonly-used tools are discussed in the order in which they are typically applied in practice.

1. Precise Problem Statement. Expressing a problem in vague terms is relatively easy, for example, poor quality, high fixed costs, high turnover, or low motivation. Such problem statements are not sufficient. In order for the team to focus its effort, the problem must be stated precisely, optimally in quantitative terms, such as "warranty claims for the consumer product 'A' line have been 25% above average for the last 60 days." The precise problem statement should specify the essence of the problem, the work area involved, the time it first started (and whether it is reoccurring), and its relative importance.

2. Force Field Analysis (FFA). This creative problem formulation tool can help teams identify the positive and negative forces affecting a desired state and provide a starting point for solving the problem. First, the team indicates the current, worst, and desired state. Next it identifies the driving forces leading to the desired situation. Then it identifies the restraining forces impending the desired state. The team graphically illustrates the magnitudinal impact of the driving forces by arrows of different lengths on a force field analysis chart. Finally the team develops an action plan to achieve the desired state. An example of a force field analysis chart for our problem of increased warranty claims is shown in Figure 3.1.

3. Brainstorming. Frequently the next step in problem solving and a well-known creative technique to expand thinking

Figure 3.1

Force Field Analysis

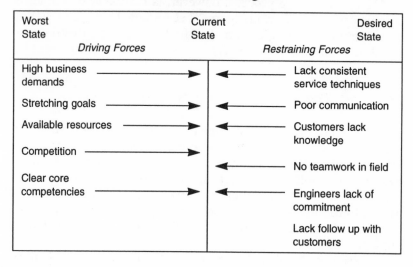

Worst State	Current State	Desired State
Driving Forces		Restraining Forces
High business demands ⟶	◀	Lack consistent service techniques
Stretching goals ⟶	◀	Poor communication
Available resources ⟶	◀	Customers lack knowledge
Competition ⟶	◀	No teamwork in field
Clear core competencies ⟶	◀	Engineers lack of commitment
		Lack follow up with customers

and quickly generate new ideas is brainstorming. After stating the problem, the team starts to generate a list of potential causes, which can lead to the generation of possible solutions later in the process. The rules for brainstorming are simple: every team member participates, ideas can be seemingly outrageous, quantity is desired, no criticism or immediate evaluation should be given, and participants should be brief and utilize their knowledge in the specific area addressed (Rawlinson 1981). Brainstorming sessions produce lists of suggestions that should be systematically analyzed using the storyboard technique.

4. Storyboarding. After a brainstorming session, this technique can be used to logically portray ideas. Storyboarding is intended to enrich group communication and promote group consensus. The brainstorming ideas are listed and then logically clustered into general categories, such as those traditionally used by Japanese quality circles: manpower, methods, machinery, and materials. Ideas clustered into groups call for a common approach and similar resources. Figure 3.2 gives an example of a storyboard for the warranty problem. An extension of the storyboarding technique is a cause-and-effect diagram.

5. Cause-And-Effect Diagram. One of the favorite techniques of Japanese quality circles is also known as the Ishikawa

Figure 3.2

Storyboarding

Manpower	Methods
engineers' lack customer sensitivity	inflexible service hours
lack follow up with customer	lack consistent service operating procedures
servicemen not 100% competent	documentation incomplete
poor communication in field	complaints drag on
	bad manuals
Machinery	Materials
equipment failure	lack of spare parts
customer do not know how to use equipment properly	parts of poor quality
	shipping shortages
pre-start check inconsistent	parts specifications inaccurate

Diagram or Fishbone Exercise. The diagram gives a graphical representation of the relationship between the problem and its causes. This tool allows the team to visualize the problem and understand the importance of thinking in terms of processes. It also helps in understanding the relationship among causes and distinguishing between factors of prime importance and those of secondary importance. To build this diagram, the team first generates the problem causes by collecting data (objective) and brainstorming (subjective). The team then writes the identified problem on the right part of the diagram and the major cause categories (the form Ms) on the left under the appropriate categories. Note in Figure 3.3 that the diagram resembles the shape of a fishbone.

6. Nominal Group Technique. Prioritizing causes of the problem required input from each team member, ensuring that the team is focused on a common issue and building consensus.

Figure 3.3
Cause and Effect Diagram

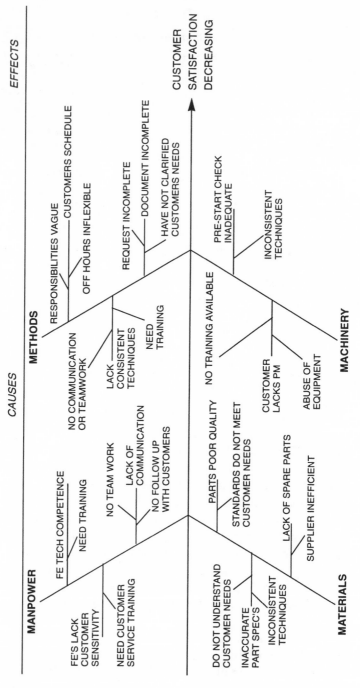

The nominal group technique generates input from each member by requiring each team member to rank the causes of the problem from the most to the least significant. The ratings are then compiled and discussed until team members reach a consensus on the key causes. This technique should be supported by the use of the Pareto chart.

7. Pareto Chart. The term "Pareto principle" was coined by Joseph Juran after a nineteenth-century Italian economist, who found that a large share of total wealth was owned by relatively few people, while most people owned a very small share of wealth. Juran extended this principle into management science, in which he found that most problems are caused by a small number of key factors. Specifically, he found that 80% of undesirable effects are caused by 20% of possible causes. The Pareto chart is applied in the following way: data are collected on each potential cause of problems, for example, scrap, rework, maintenance time, customer inquiries, lack of spare parts, customer misuse of equipment, and incomplete documentation. The potential causes are then organized so that the most frequent (highest cost) cause is placed on the left, with the other causes placed in descending order of frequency. The final chart typically looks like the one shown in Figure 3.4.

Figure 3.4

Pareto Chart of Warranty Claims

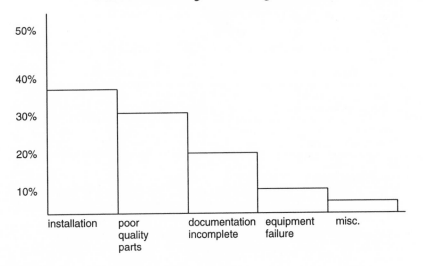

8. Solution Impact Analysis. When the vital causes of the problem are diagnosed, the team can develop solutions and analyze the significance of each solution's impact on the underlying causes. As with the nominal group technique, group consensus is sought in judging the potential impact of particular solutions. The final outcome of such an analysis is shown in Table 3.1. We can see that Solution 1 is judged to have the greatest impact (27 points), with Solution 3 having the least impact (23 points). We can apply more sophisticated calculation methods to the matrix, such as calculating the weighted averages of impacts made by varying solutions, and introducing the cost of a solution as a factor.

9. Action Plan. Up until now we have concentrated our attention on diagnostic tools. The action plan must follow the diagnosis, clearly stipulating the goals that the team wants to achieve (what is to be done?); the solutions applied (how will it be achieved?); responsibility and accountability regarding implementation (who does what), along with a timetable and measurement criteria for monitoring progress. If the solutions are costly it is natural that the group will seek management approval. In this case, the action plan will take the form of a "business plan" that the self-managed group will try to 'sell' to managers in a similar fashion, as an entrepreneur sells his business concept to banks or venture capital firms. Management will challenge the recommendations and proposed action plan.

Table 3.1 Solution Impact Matrix

	Solution 1	Solution 2	Solution 3
Cause 1 Importance = 35%	H	M	M
Cause 2 Importance = 30%	H	H	H
Cause 3 Importance = 20%	—	L	M
Cause 4 Importance = 10%	L	M	—
Total	27	24	23

* *Note:* We assumed that H (High Impact) is equal numerically to 40; M (Medium Impact) to 20, and L (Low Impact) to 10. Therefore the total value of the Solution 1 = 35*40 + 0.30*40 + 10*10 = 27 etc.

The nine tools that we have discussed are used by all types of teams everywhere—in the United States, Europe, and Pacific Rim countries. They have proved to be both simple and powerful. These techniques encourage systematic problem solving with precise problem formulation, careful choice of data collection and analysis techniques, and creative formulation of solutions.

MAIN TYPES OF SELF-MANAGED TEAMS

The main types of self-managed teams are production teams, quality circles, and problem-solving teams. These three types are organized for varying purposes and function in different ways. We will discuss each of the types in greater detail.

Production Teams

According to Hackman (1990: 107), self-managed production teams "begin with a set of raw materials and use tools and technology to transform them into outputs. The objectives of production teams typically involve the predictable and efficient creation of high quality products. Consequently, these teams tend to focus on ways to minimize unexplained variations in the production process through increasingly standardized operating procedures. Teams exercise initiative in pushing back the frontier between the uncontrollable and controllable."

Self-managed production teams are flexible, adaptive, and capable of collective learning. To help foster team members' motivation, group tasks should have three properties: self-containment, autonomy, and verifiability. (Hackman and Oldham 1980). In most cases, however, a technology is designed to be utilized by a person rather than by a team. The layout of a typical assembly line or production line is a case in point. Thus, in order to introduce self-managed teams, the production process must be designed to incorporate production teams. The experience of Chiptronics and Albany International illustrate this redesign.

Chiptronics. In the Chiptronics semiconductor factory studied by Abramis (1990: 450), the introduction of teamwork required the following steps:

1. Employees working next to each other on an assembly line were divided into groups of three to seven people.

2. The production technology was redesigned to enable most team members to be grouped in U-shaped configurations.

3. Supervisors were renamed "group advisors."

4. Group advisors were charged with managing production groups as well as individuals.

5. Employees were given both individual feedback and feedback about team performance as a whole.

6. All workers were instructed as to the new team-based organization.

Albany International. At Albany International, construction of the new East Greenbush Plant provided an opportunity for the dramatic redesign of processes and structures. As one of AI's executives told *American Papermaker* (1990: 63): "the lack of walls and offices on the factory floor underscores the fact that there are no departments at East Greenbush, but rather a series of processes that are run as a team concept." Five layers of supervision were eliminated, enabling employees working in production to communicate with each other in an effort to produce better product more efficiently. The manufacturing plant is run by four multi-skilled teams: Blue, Red, Orange, and Green, made up of 30–35 people each. The teams were given names derived from colors so as to avoid any sort of ranking.

Team Leader

The team leader coordinates the activities of team members, who trade off between the day and night shifts on a monthly basis. Good communication at shift changes is critical for ensuring smooth operations at all hours of operation (O'Brien 1989).

The key issue in building effective self-managed production teams is to constantly keep in mind the needs of the final customer and avoid allowing the internal logic of the production process to impose its own standards of efficiency for its own sake. As Frank Schmeller, Senior Vice President of Albany International, stated, "Doing things right is what AI sees as a key to its future success. This refers to 'flattening' the organization; communicating horizontally as well as vertically; focusing on the customer's process; anticipating customer's and supplier's respective processes and problems" (*American Papermaker* 1990: 63). As mentioned in its company literature, AI's company culture is driven by a mission to "operate as a world class manufacturer of superior products and services, which exceed customer expectations." It goes on to describe the three quality values that drive the East Greenbush operation:

1. Customer focus.
2. Process management. (continuous improvement and innovation of all processes, products and services)
3. Employee empowerment. (the most important source of improvement and innovation comes from making customer focus and process improvement the right and responsibility of every employee)

Skillful leadership plays a key role in building and operating self-managed production teams. The leadership role is often played by more than one person in the position of "team leader," "team coordinator," or "team advisor." Some of the people playing leadership roles are elected by the team members, as in the team coordinators at Chiptronics (Abramis 1990: 457). Some are appointed by the management, as with the captain leading the airline cockpit crews studied by Ginett (1990), or even self-appointed, as in the case of the "engineering genius and social misfit" described by Barry (1991).

Leadership Functions

Barry (1991: 36) identifies four types of leadership functions required for effective operation of self-managed work groups: envisioning, organizing, advising, and spanning.

- Envisioning involves creating new and compelling visions. Leaders should encourage frame-breaking thinking, facilitate new goal formation and discovery of conceptual links among different ideas, systems, and subsystems.
- Organizing brings order to the group's life and focuses on details, deadlines, efficiency and structure. The leader's organizing skills are especially important on the shop floor of relatively well structured situations, where conflicts

sometimes occur between innovation and order. Even highly mature groups have problems coping with such conflicts, especially when these two conflicting values are represented by different "sub-leaders."

- Advising helps improve the socio-psychological strength of the group, and requires the leader to be sensitive to the group's energy levels, emotional states, conflict potential, and possible solutions. The leader will need to anticipate problems that could lead to a decrease in morale, member satisfaction, and ultimately, performance.

- Spanning leadership focuses on the links between the group and outside groups and individuals. This leadership function enables smooth coordination and the group's contribution to a larger system. Spanning leadership is easier and more effective when the larger system (corporation) is organized as a network. The network could be based on interconnected self-managed groups and cross-managed teams on the levels of top management, middle management, and operations. Spanning leadership provides loosely structured networks with the required degree of homogeneity.

The semiconductor manufacturing group at Chiptronics (Abramis 1990) was tightly linked to other people and groups in the production operation. Horizontal links with other groups were well defined. The production group was a customer of the group that preceded it, while its own customer was the team coming on during the next shift. The team advisor was performing the spanning leadership function by managing such horizontal links. Vertical linkages, also close, were also managed by the team advisor. All information relevant to production, such as feedback about performance or changes in production targets, was passed to team members through the team advisor. Team advisor also served as a link between the production group and people from departments outside the group structure, such as the maintenance and engineering personnel.

The distributed leadership model proposed by Barry (1991) implies that different leadership roles are performed by different people in different circumstances and at different stages of the group life cycle. The group's survival and continued performance requires the continual presence of adequate leadership potential to allow leadership functions to be carried out effectively. In teams involved in more simple and more structured tasks all four leadership functions tend to be performed by one or two people as at Chiptronics (Abramis 1990). Larger teams performing more complex tasks require a correspondingly more complex leadership structure.

Productivity Enhancements

Data collected by Abramis (1990: 460) point to four ways in which self-managed production teams enhance productivity:

- decentralization of quality control mechanisms
- cross-training to enhance knowledge and increase flexibility
- improved communication among production workers
- higher employee morale

An *Industry Week* survey conducted in 1990 indicated three benefits from self-managed work groups:

- improved group involvement and performance
- positive morale
- sense of ownership and commitment to the product (Verespej 1990: 30)

By pushing decision-making downward and allowing those closest to the work resolve issues affecting their work processes, decisions can be made more quickly, with more direct response to the real issues. Voluntary participation in improving work processes has risen dramatically at Albany International's East Greenbush plant. This enthusiasm has been evident during team meetings. Team meetings are small gatherings of 5–11 people, who are encouraged to participate actively, ask questions, make suggestions, and present data. Teams (groups) have the authority to act upon suggestions and ideas supported by the group, giving the employees a sense that their input is valued and may be incorporated into the work process.

Members of self-managed production teams are given opportunities for cross-training. Production workers value the idea of cross-training because it both creates a potential opportunity to switch jobs and reduces the monotony of their jobs. Cross-training also increases the group's accumulated knowledge, skill level, and flexibility in dealing with crisis situations (such as production bottlenecks, industrial disasters, and absenteeism). It also enhances communication and personal relationships among group members (Abramis 1990: 461).

Both the flat organizational structure of production groups and the necessity to coordinate both internally and with other groups makes team-based industrial structures extremely information intensive. There is an added emphasis on informal and unstructured aspects of communication (Wellins and George 1991). At the East Greenbush plant area meetings are held weekly on the factory floor to inform employees about changes in procedures and equipment, upcoming new product trials, recent equipment problems, results of field runs, financial or production results, and so forth.

Self-managed production teams are created not only to encourage a more stable flow of production but also to complete "one-time" projects. The projects are unique, such as with the compressor production line start-up studied by Eisenstat (1990). In this case, a production group itself has to be produced along with the intended tangible result. The materials from which the company produced the group included a facility, pieces of technology (not all of it in place when the group was started), individual team members (also not all in place from the beginning), and a checklist specifying in detail what the team was supposed to accomplish. "An iterative transformation process based on these materials resulted in an intact, functioning work team, with members ready and able to work together to produce high quality compression parts. The compressor team was, quite literally, the product of a production process at Fairfield" (Hackman 1990: 471).

Creating and sustaining self-managed production teams is not an easy undertaking. When creating and sustaining such complex social systems (even quite small ones), managers are faced with several serious problems. These problems include: "personnel and personality conflicts, an unwillingness on the part of managers to give up their power, worker distrust of management, and fear on the part of supervisors that they might lose their jobs . . . Another obstacle for self-directed teams is company's reluctance to make investments to help work teams succeed...The other problem: finding workers with the right mental attitude to work in teams (Verespej 1990: 31–32).

According to Dumaine (1990: 54) success requires the following: "functional chimneys must be broken down and middle managers persuaded to lend their time, people and resources to other functions for the good of the entire corporation."

Hackman (1990: 475) points out that self-managed teams have a tendency to develop and sustain an "inward" orientation. They focus to a much greater extent on internal transactions rather than on external transactions with the clients, suppliers, and so forth. "Paradoxically, it appears that a team's external transactions may both spur and fuel its internal development. Interactions with outsiders present problems and opportunities whose resolution can help a team to clarify its own identity, elaborate its norms, and refine its performance strategies. Without such interactions, a team may be unable to keep pushing forward its own development as a performing unit" (Hackman 1990: 475–76).

Self-managed production teams require constant care and maintenance. They are sensitive to personnel changes at the middle-management level. The delicate internal and external balance is difficult to maintain.

Quality Circles

Quality circles are undoubtedly the best-known and the most publicized form of teamwork on the shop floor level. Their renown most likely results from their widespread use and unquestionable contribution to Japan's rise from a manufacturer of low quality goods to one producing at the world's highest standards. It has been estimated that in the early 1980s, approximately ten million Japanese workers participated in over one million quality circles. This movement is widely imitated in many countries, especially in the United States (Mohr and Mohr 1983).

Definition.   A quality circle is a small group of workers performing similar kinds of work in the same company. Quality circles ideally consist of approximately eight workers, but can have between three and fifteen. The group is formed on a voluntary basis and meets regularly, usually once a week for an hour, to identify, analyze and solve problems group members encounter in their work. Upon finding a solution to a particular problem, circle members present it to management for approval. Once recommendations are approved they are implemented by the quality circle.

Objectives. Ishikawa (1985: 33) identifies three main objectives for organizing QCs:

1. To foster study groups in which foremen and workers together study the quality control problems and programs.
2. To apply the results of their study to their workshops to achieve more effective management and improvements in the work environment.
3. To expand and enrich the personality of foremen and workers.

Other authors (Mohr & Mohr 1983: 13) and experts formulate objectives of QCs in a similar way.

Principles

Authors writing about QCs usually provide a list of the principles of QC activities, containing key words. Some of these lists are quite extensive, for example the one formulated by Ishikawa (1985: 33–34) consists of thirty items. Our list of QC principles (based in part on Ishikawa's) is more brief:

1. Voluntary. Quality circles should be formed on a strictly voluntary basis on the workshop level ("workshopism" or starting with the workshop).
2. Wide participation. Quality circles are a group activity meant to include everyone, including workers who tend to be indifferent. It should broaden people's horizons, enrich their personalities, and strengthen their will to excel.
3. Incorporation in Work Activities. Circle activities must be incorporated into ordinary work activities.
4. Increasingly Complex Problem Solving. Quality circles should start with a focus on concrete, immediate, and smaller problems. The ability to solve more difficult problems will be acquired gradually through guidance,

training, and support. Members will appreciate the pleasure of solving problems.

5. Implementation. Implementation of recommendations should remain within the power of the workgroup on the workshop level.

6. Grassroots. All participants should be fully involved. The initiative should not be taken by only supervisors, leaders, foremen, or advisors. All members should participate.

7. Open Discussion. Discussions should be open and frank. Group members should learn how to listen to their co-members with an open mind.

Support

Planning a QC program required support and active participation both from unions and from management. Managers must be persuaded that the program is needed; they must understand their purpose and objectives. Management must assess the company situation to judge whether the timing is right to initiate a QC program, and whether adequate resources can be allocated to support the program. Once management supports the initiation of a QC program, it must win union support by presenting to the union the benefits of "working smarter."

Steering Committee

Once management has decided to start a QC program within the organization, a steering committee must be formed. It should be composed of six to twelve members representing each of the main functional areas of the organization and the various hierarchical levels. For example, (Mohr and Mohr 1983: 46–47) at Hewlett-Packard's Data Systems Division, a steering committee for its QC program was established. The committee was composed of three first-level supervisors (Engineering Services Supervisor, Technical Support Manager, Production Engineering Manager), two second-level managers (Section Manager, Cost Accounting Manager), one third-level manager

(Quality/Productivity Training Manager), and seven nonmanagerial employees (Secretary, Printed Circuit Board Assembler, Machine Operator, Expediter, Engineer, Personnel Administrator, Production Control Scheduler).

The Steering Committee should provide guidelines for the QC program. The written guidelines address the following four questions:

1. What do we want to achieve through the QC program, i.e., what is its general purpose?
2. What specific objectives is the program intended to achieve?
3. What are the rules by which the circles will operate?
4. How are circles to be formed?

Guidelines answering the questions above should be distributed as an official company document.

The Steering Committee should also decide whether the company requires a quality-circle program coordinator. Larger programs are usually supported by a full-time person. The program coordinator provides a liaison between those participating in the QC program and both internal and external support elements. The program coordinator should be skilled in participative decision making and strongly support the QC movement.

After resolving the general problems, the Steering Committee can develop a start-up plan. Such a plan should state the initial number of QCs and their location within the company structure. The plan should also list the evaluation criteria of the QCs' activities, as well as the process for selecting and training circle leaders, facilitators, and members. Formulation of the start-up plan provides a good opportunity for the steering committee to practice consensus management.

Another important element of the start-up plan is the program budget. The budget has three elements:

• Start-up costs. Money for initial training and preparation necessary to start the QC program (including consultants, printing of training materials, and so forth).
• Costs of participants' time. Budget to cover the value of time spent by facilitator, leaders, and the employee team members.

• Implementation costs. Budget for the implementation of solutions formulated by the QCs. It includes expenses for materials and equipment as well as rewards for ideas. Some companies give financial rewards, while in others QC members are rewarded under "normal" productivity or suggestion incentive programs. In some companies, intrinsic and symbolic rewards are more appropriate.

The International Association of Quality Circles conservatively estimates a 3:1 return on investment ratio for QCs based on its members' experience. Benefits resulting from a QC program are not free: financial resources have to be allocated to its implementation.

Pilot Program

After the planning phase, the Steering Committee implements a pilot program. The pilot program has a key importance for the future proliferation of the QC movement in the company. It should allow for experimentation with the new structure and for successful promotion to the majority of company employees.

Training.   Once a decision is reached as to the location of the first circles, a training program for the facilitator and leaders should be started immediately. There are four options available for training:

1. Hiring an external consultant
2. Enrolling in off-site training courses offered by the IAQC or other specialized organizations
3. Buying an off-the-shelf training package
4. Developing training materials within the organization (Mohr and Mohr 1983: 61)

Leadership Selection.   Selection of the program facilitator and leaders should be based on clear-cut criteria.

The role of a facilitator is often compared to that of a midwife: helping members to give birth to their own ideas. Both part-time and full-time facilitators are used. Full-time facilitators are usually behavioral science specialists in group dynamics hired from outside the organization. Usually they serve up to fifteen circles. Part-time facilitators are often volunteers from the ranks of middle management. Even if he or she is not a professional group specialist, a part-time facilitator provides a useful link between middle management and the activities of the quality circles. They are more likely than the full-time facilitator to add significantly to the level of enthusiasm for and within the circles.

The leader is responsible for the content of the QC activities. he or she should ensure that a focus is kept on important problems and that the agenda is set collectively. Leaders provide guidance, and, at the same time, participate in circle's activities on equal terms with the others. Work area supervisors are the most likely candidates for the pilot program. They should demonstrate strong communication skills (especially the ability to listen), an ability to organize collective work within relatively rigid time constraints, show respect for the team members, and practice a participative management style.

To select quality-circle members, the employees working in a given leader's area of responsibility are invited to attend an introductory presentation. Afterwards, they are given one week to consider the program and decide if they want to volunteer. A predetermined number is selected on a "first come, first served" basis; eventually a waiting list for a second circle is established. Training of the circle members is done by their own leader and facilitator and helps to build the "team spirit." Such training usually takes two four-hour sessions.

Hewlett-Packard's management has given active support to the circles' activities and committed itself to the program's success. At one of HP's divisions, management support to the quality-circles movement included the following (Mohr and Mohr 1983: 76–77):

1. Providing employees time to participate in QC activities.

2. Allocating time for management presentations and casual visits to the meetings.

3. Providing timely response to the circles' proposals.

4. Presenting and praising QCs' activities at functional and interdivisional meetings.

5. Considering quality circles' request for financial support.

6. Providing feedback to the Steering Committee regarding problems with and praise for the QCs.

7. Allowing rewards and recognition to be intrinsic; not stimulating competition.

8. Not limiting QC support activities to the list above.

Review of the pilot program should provide a well-grounded answer to the question of whether the program should be continued and expanded. It should also provide guidelines for the program's full fledged implementation, thus helping to avoid pitfalls and mistakes.

Cultural Influences

Implementation of the QC program is undoubtedly affected by culture and takes somewhat different forms in various contexts such as different countries and companies. When analyzing quality circles in the US and in Japan, Ishikawa (1985: 36–37) discovered several important differences.

In the United States, quality circles are more formal in character and often are organized as formal staff organizations. Supervisors often become circle leaders. Middle management takes a lead in the movement. In Japan, circles are more similar to informal groups of workers. Workers are circle leaders,while managers become advisors or consultants. Workers often join the circles as a result of informal group pressure.

Activities of quality circles in the US are often led through the initiative of management. Meetings are generally held during work; otherwise, workers receive overtime compensation. Most incentive schemes are offered to individual workers. Difficulties arise with attempts to increase the duration of activities; thus, quality circles ten to become involved in "ad hoc" activities. In Japanese quality circles, workers play a more active role. They more often take the initiative in selecting both the content and method of the circle's work. Meetings are held both during and after work hours; no overtime is paid. Benefits generated by the proposals are distributed in the form of bonuses to all employees. Circle activities have a longer duration because of their truly voluntary nature.

Problems with Quality Circles

Mohr and Mohr (1983) indicate several problems and pitfalls associated with the quality circle movement: QCs should be installed for "people-building," not for "people-using." A narrowly pragmatic view of the QC as a simple instrument for improving quality and productivity often leads to failure. Intelligent, educated, and informed employees quickly discover the true intentions of the management and indicate their displeasure of being manipulated. When the QC movement is perceived as an opportunity for development and self-realization, positive attitudes are more likely to prevail. The QC program should be perceived as a long term investment, not as a panacea or a "quick fix."

Quality circles must be voluntary. Unrealistic expectations on the part of circle members, mainly due to inadequate training and pressure from management to joint the circle, trigger disillusionment and sap workers' motivation.

Without management's full and visible support, the QC movement's desired outcomes are not likely to materialize. At Honeywell, Incorporated, middle managers are specially trained to reinforce circle leaders' skills, which helps to diagnose problems with group dynamics and assist them in correcting such problems.

Quality-circle burnout occurs when the novelty of problem solving wears off and frustrations accumulate because of the circles' inability to solve problems in a timely manner. Proper scheduling and efficient conduct of the meetings can easily become another source of problems.

Ishikawa (1985: 36–37) compares problems encountered by quality circles in the United States and in Japan: In the United States, unions tend to treat QCs as another platform for their activities. The duration of activities are short, due to lay-offs and a high turnover rate, which makes long-term investment in training questionable. Top management tends to expect excessive short-term gains. American individualism makes teamwork difficult. Finally, it is especially difficult to gain support from middle management.

In Japan, securing the participation of all workers is still difficult. The power of the Steering Committee is often not enough to ensure quick implementation of the program. Education and training are often insufficient. As in the United States, participation by middle management is often not satisfactory. Often having a number of meetings still does not bring satisfactory results.

The success or failure of the quality circles depends upon proper use of simple problem-solving techniques we have already discussed (such as storyboard, cause and effect diagram, Pareto charts, and so forth), all of which are well known and described in the related literature (Mohr and Mohr 1983; Rawlinson 1981; Ishikawa 1976; Adams 1974). These techniques should be incorporated into the collective problem solving process. This requires members' involvement, proper guidance, and adequate training. The combination of these three conditions is not easy to achieve in practice. Only mature, sophisticated organizations with stabilized and highly motivated core personnel can hope to achieve this combination.

Problem Solving Teams

At Albany International, problem-solving teams concentrate on process improvement. A process, as defined by Walton (1990: 109), is "a series of actions which repeatedly come together to transform inputs provided by a supplier into outputs received by a customer." A business can be perceived as a network of interdependent value-adding processes. Benson (1992: 28) defines process improvement as "the practice of continually working with the cumulative steps involved to make the process more efficient, more productive, most cost-effective, and easier to use, while making what it produces (a sales order, a manufactured product, an accounting report, and so forth) of consistently higher quality." Process improvement must be based on problem solving. It is clearly visible in the guidelines of the Hospital Corporation of America. Its system for process improvement is called FOCUS-PDCA:

Find a process to improve

Organize a team that knows the process

Clarify current knowledge of the process

Understand causes of process variation

Select the process improvement

Plan the improvement and continue data collection

Do the improvement, data collection, and analysis

Check the results and lessons learned

Act to hold the gain and continue to improve the process
  (Walton 1990: 108–109)

According to Persisco (1989: 36), the process of quality improvement includes identifying the customers and their requirements; defining the current process to meet their needs; determining the problems in the process; analyzing the problem using problem solving techniques; improving the process; and monitoring and planning for continuous improvement.

At the Press Fabrics Division at Albany International, fourteen teams were involved in process improvement. They were typically composed of 4–6 members and a team leader who, in some cases, also served as the technical advisor.

Process Mapping

Teams often use process mapping as a problem-solving technique. Process mapping is "a visual tool that displays in one graphic presentation a complete project or plan, the major elements, and how they interrelate over time" (Sibbet and O'Hara 1991: 29). Graphic forms represent a powerful communication instrument, enabling group members to understand the same problem definition and to better understand and remember the problem. It enhances communication between workers and management. General Electric has found from its own experience that "when a process is mapped, GE has often for the first time—the ability to manage an operation in a coherent way from start to finish" (Stewart 1991: 48).

1. Work Flow Diagrams.   Several types of process maps are used. The most common are work flow diagrams and flow charts. A work flow diagram is "a picture of the movements of people, materials, documents or information in a process. It is created by tracing these movements on a sketch of the floor plan or some similar map of the work space" (Scholtes 1988: 22). Such diagrams can clearly indicate which elements of the process need improving and why. For example, bottlenecks can be detected when the flow of material throughout the process is properly represented on the diagram.

2. Flow Chart.   A flow chart is a pictorial representation of all the steps or stages in a process. Flow charts are used for "defining supplier-customer relationships, describing the process and making it tangible, standardizing procedures, designing a new process or modifying an existing process, identifying complexity or opportunities for improvement" (Moen et al.

1991: 16). The goal of the flow chart is to describe the process as it currently exists. Flow charts enable a group solving problems related to the process improvement to have a visual representation of the process and to better understand its logic. Flow charts can also be used to train personnel about the proper working of the process, about the means available for its control, and about potential areas of improvement (Stevick, 1990: 73).

General Electric Programs

At General Electric, an enormous employee involvement program has been set in motion by the legendary CEO Jack Welch. This program consists of two elements: training in problem-solving techniques and work-out sessions.

1. Problem Solving Training. According to Perry (1991: 68): "Seventy-five percent of the people who will be working in the year 2000 are already on the job. These people are being asked to handle new technologies and expanded responsibilities and many are ill-prepared to do so." The changing nature of job responsibilities requires organizations to constantly train and retrain their workforce. As Bob Huff, a GE blue-collar worker, says: "At GE Aircraft Engines, 11,000 of the 38,000 employees have already taken a two-day course in problem solving. One thing people bring away from the class...is the sense that they can control their day and make a difference. Before, the hourly people felt like every time we walked through the gate we checked our brains at the guard shack. So this is starting to tap into untapped resources, which is neat" (Perry 1991: 71).

Every week, throughout GE, people are formed into groups of different sizes (in some instances as many as 50 to 150 employees), picked from all levels of the company, to develop ideas intended to make GE more competitive. Annually, about 20,000 to 25,000 GE employees attend two- or three-day work-outs.

2. Work-Outs. The building blocks of work-outs consist of five levels of the group problem solving process:

- Level I—Town Meetings
- Level II—Productivity Best Practices Workshops

- Level III—Integration with on-going quality and continuous improvement (CI) efforts
- Level IV—Customer–Supplier Work-outs
- Level V—"?" – An evolving process on the road to becoming the most competitive enterprise on Earth (Work-Out 1991:2)

Level I: Town Meeting. The overriding objective of the Town Meetings is to maintain an internal focus. This is accomplished by encouraging spontaneous "bureaucracy bashing," removing non value-added work, freeing up and energizing individuals, valuing the ideas of the workers closest to the physical work process ("management doesn't always know best"), giving individuals "voice" by creating a forum for dialogue, encouraging novel and creative expressions of ideas, and choosing a cross section of the company to execute those ideas. In some cases, external consultants specializing in group dynamics are invited to help the process.

Level II: Productivity Best Practices Workshop. In contrast to the first level, the Productivity Best Practices Workshops have as their overriding objective the maintenance of an external focus. Such a focus requires performing environmental scanning by the Corporate Business Planning and Development Department to bring the best practices of other companies to the General Electric training center in Crotonville, N.Y. The Best Practices Workshops bring the best of other companies to Crotonville, stimulating thinking and increasing awareness. In recent years, General Electric completed a series of Best Practices Studies to examine the management techniques of ten world-class companies, ranging from AMP and Xerox to Chaparral Steel and Honda. All ten companies accepted GE's request to study their best practices, in return for a similarly detailed insight into GE's management methods. The idea behind Level II is to solve thousands of problems having one thing in common: adaptation of others' best practices to GE's management on all levels in all units and "finding a better way...everyday."

Level III: Integration. The major objective of the third level of work-outs is to obtain a high level of integration with ongoing quality and continuous improvement efforts. At this level, the idea emphasized is that "It's not about words, it's about ends." This action focus demands a shift from idea generation to the identification of specific processes for implementing problem solutions, within the context of the company goals and overall company policies.

Level IV: Customer - Supplier Work-outs. The goal of this level is to integrate suppliers and customers more closely with GE and to develop a partnership through intensive joint problem solving. Within the framework of "boundaryless relationships," GE views customers/suppliers as one system defined as "external stakeholders."

Level V: ?. The main objective of the fifth level: "?" is to identify emerging issues and "weak signals." The focus is on measurements and systems, which can help GE in the future to become "the most competitive enterprise on earth."

Work-out Phases. According to GE's company literature there are six phases of a GE workout session:

1. Group start up
   - mission, goals and objectives
   - operating principles (how team will work together, make decisions, resolve conflicts, give everyone an opportunity to express opinions, agree on solutions etc.)
2. Data collection (information dump)
   - perception sharing
   - brainstorming (what's working and what's not)
   - input from colleagues back home
   - "RAMMP analysis" - reduction or elimination of unnecessary reports, approvals, meetings, measures and policies
3. Data sorting and analysis
   - what is critical to fix?
   - storyboarding to group or cluster data
   - further clarification of data from team members
   - visionary/outcome thinking (what the group would rather see)
4. Problem selection and analysis
   - problem definition and analysis
   - problem prioritizing
   - tools like fishbone diagrams and force field analysis

5. Solution selection

- what will solve the problem?
- how does group knows it will work?
- solution impact matrix
- projected cost/impact analysis
- contingency diagram

6. Recommendation formulation

- action plan
- potential obstacles
- implementation

Most of the problem solving techniques used at GE have already been described in more detail. As we have noted, the main advantages of these techniques are simplicity and the ability to trigger group dynamics to promote collective creativity. Problem-solving groups try to make the best use of the company's human potential; improve the level of innovation; and remain sensitive to the company's opportunities, threats, and weaknesses.

Key Success Factors of Self-Managed Teams

Benefits of self-managed teams cannot be taken for granted. As we established at the beginning of this chapter, successful teams must have a common objective, unique interests, and a culture of mutual trust and respect. In addition, each member's concerns and contributions must be clearly communicated and appropriately integrated into the team's performance. Considerable effort is needed to create such conditions. Hackman (1990) identifies three groups of such conditions:

- Team structure that promotes competent work on the task
- Organization context that supports and reinforces excellence
- Available expert coaching and process assistance

Team Structure

Common factors of team structure are task structure, norms regulating member behavior, and team composition.

A clearly formulated task with some so-called "missionary" flavor enabling the members to share responsibility and accountability enhances team performance. British Airways, for instance, created its "Customer First Team," in which team members were instructed to look for ways to improve the airline's services. In addition, the task structure should enable team members to learn quickly how well they are doing on the job. In this respect Hewlett Packard has been using a system called "the return map," enabling individuals to assess how well they are doing and what should be done to improve performance (House and Price 1991).

Norms regulating members' behavior develop as a part of the organizational culture. These norms are strongly influenced by the national culture. A somewhat extreme example comes from Kiocera's in Kagoshima, the southern island of Kyushu, where young employees live in dorms. In the morning, foremen salute the plant manager as they report the number of workers present. To make the work groups more competitive and further strengthen group spirit, the groups compete with one another in intramural sports during off-hours (Bylinsky 1990: 86).

Team composition involves the skills and interpersonal relations of the group members as well as cultural and ethnic differences. For example, when Motorola installed one of its plants in Mexico, it realized some important cultural differences between American and Mexican workers. Management consultants helped to identify some key differences. Americans are more inclined to take the initiative. They generally take individual responsibility and consider failure personal. In contrast, Mexicans prefer to work in groups so that they can share equally both failure and success. Further, the most important values for Mexican workers were successively family, religion, and work: they tend to live for the day. Americans are more future oriented.

Knowledge of these differences enabled Motorola's management to build high-performing, mixed autonomous production teams able to cut in half the cycle time of semiconductor products manufacturing (Baning and Wintermantel 1991: 55).

Organizational Context

The organizational context of the production teams includes the reward system, the educational system, and the information system.

Reward System. Gain sharing is the most widely suggested method for motivating group members. Such group-based reward systems have positive implications for improving the work atmosphere as well as both employee and company profits. Hinckley's CEO, John Marshall, describes the gain-sharing system: "Our goal in putting in place a gain sharing plan was to establish an environment at Hinckley in which ownership, management and the productive crew all were members of the same team. When we produce the top quality work in the most productive way, everyone benefits. If we have problems of any sort, it should be a concern of every member of the team" (Paulsen 1989: 17). In this way the importance of teamwork is reinforced. People feel themselves to be members of a team as well as "members" of a company. "A productive company providing superior services and sharing its success with its employees is a team that is hard to beat" (Paulsen 1989: 19).

Educational System. Training employees in multiple skills brings more flexibility to the companies, making job assignments and the redesign of activities easier. Training also improves the attitude of the employees toward the organization and increases the motivational level that results from more responsibility, creativity, and initiative on the job. As one American manager of employee relations puts it: "We're trying to change the way people manage their work—from a traditional base that's been around for forty years to one in which we encourage people not to check their brain at the door" (Rohan 1990: 14).

Information System. Teamwork requires changes in communication patterns. In a traditional work organization, direct communication from the shop floor level, relevant to the work performance, is often missing. Any problems that occur are reported to the bosses, who in turn report them to a concerned department. In self-managed production teams the communication is seldom downward—as greater decision power is delegated—but appears to be upward, to report serious problems or to give suggestions, to ask for or suggest changes. The communication is also mostly horizontal, implying that decisions are mostly made among team members, and that problems are solved that way too.

Expert Coaching and Process Assistance

Self-managed teams are not always able to take full advantage of positive performance conditions, especially at the earlier stages of group formation. In order to enhance a group's performance, a leader, consultant(s), or facilitator(s) is/are needed. Specific kinds of help that might be provided according to Hackman (1990:12) include the following:

- Assistance in minimizing the coordination and motivation decrements and in building commitment to the group and its task
- Assistance in avoiding inappropriate "weighing" of different individuals' ideas and contributions and in learning how to share their expertise and develop the appropriate repertory of skills
- Assistance in avoiding a flawed implementation of the group process and in developing creative new ways of proceeding with the team's work

Research reported in Magjuka's article (1991/1992) indicates that all forms of teamwork are closely entwined with goal-setting processes. In order to align goal setting in complex organizations with team effort, special goal review committees must be put in place. Forty-three percent of the respondents said that their groups' activities did not include goal setting processes, while 57 percent indicated that goal setting was part of their groups' operations (Magjuka 1991/1992: 55).

Creating conditions to enhance group performance can be considered a "fine art of today's management" providing for effective implementation of the continuous improvement paradigm.

FOUR

Cross-Functional Teams

Much of the work in large organizations is now done in small groups or
teams. When those teams work badly,
as they often do, they can block even
the most talented individual from
reaching their potential. When they
work well, they can elevate the performance of ordinary mortals to extraor-
dinary heights. (Bolman and Deal,
1992: 34)

Global leaders are entering the age of the "organizational revolution of the nineties." Traditional hierarchies are being replaced
by flat, information-based organizations. They demonstrate
behavioral patterns similar to those of philharmonic orchestras,
jazz combos, spider webs, or other living, growing creatures
capable of adaptation to the environment. They are practicing
effective internal co-alignment" (Stewart 1992).

Self-managed and cross-functional teams, effectively ad-
justing to rapidly changing environments and constantly inter-
changing their members, are the back-bone of these new
structures. Therefore, an ability to generate such teams and
have them perform according to the company's overall objectives is one of the key conditions enabling the development of
a competitive advantage on the global market. These teams
also help to sustain the advantage through continuous
improvement. In chapter 3, we developed the role of the self-
managed team. Let us now turn to the nature and role of
cross-functional teams.

PURPOSE OF CROSS-FUNCTIONAL TEAMS

We have already established the generic characteristics of effective teamwork as: (1) the development of a popularly constructed and supported goal; (2) the integration of team members' unique interests, concerns and contributions; and (3) a culture of mutual respect and trust. The general purposes for developing cross-functional teams are to increase "speed to market" productivity (by eliminating barriers between parts of an organization), and process-oriented cooperation. In order to achieve these goals, cross-functional teams uniquely integrate organizational activities across an entire functional value chain.

Speed to Market

The most important market-related purpose for developing effective cross-functional teamwork is "speed to market" (Vessey, 1991; Ju and Cushman 1995). "Speed-to-market" is defined as the time elapsed between defining a product and its availability on the market. Markets based on technological innovations, fashion, or fads generously reward speed in engineering, production, sales response, and customer service, as demonstrated simultaneously in all advanced countries. This potential competitive advantage is a simple result of shrinking product life cycles and competition among leading firms. Achieving a "speed-to-market advantage" required effectively removing all artificial barriers among functional units along the firm's value chain and building effective cross-managed teams both at the top management and operational levels (Cushman and King 1995). Teams make possible the abolition of barriers, increased information sharing, and a climate of cooperation both within the organization and on the inter-organizational level involving suppliers, buyers, clients, sub-contractors and so forth.

Cross-Functional Cooperation

A second purpose of cross-functional teams is allowing for cooperation between people from different organizational units (such as R&D, production, marketing, finance, and so forth). In traditionally rigid organizations, such cross-functional cooperation is blocked. Xerox discovered this lack of cooperation:

> It is a management axiom that crabgrass grows in the cracks between departments. Purchasing buys parts cheap, but manufacturing needs them strong. Shipping moves goods in bulk, but sales promised them fast. 'I call it Palermo's law,' says Richard Palermo, a vice president for quality and transition at Xerox. 'If a problem has been bothering your company and your customers for years and it won't yield, that problem is the result of a cross-functional dispute, where nobody has total control of the whole process.' And here is Palermo's corollary: People who work in different functions hate each other. (Stewart 1992: 95)

Teams facilitate cross-functional cooperation, especially as applies to the integrative role of marketing. Many researchers have clearly demonstrated the relations between marketing and R&D, (Gupta and Wilemon 1988), marketing and production (Clare & Sanford 1984); and marketing and finance, engineering, and other functions (Bonoma 1984). Marketing people often play a key role in cross-functional teams, because they provide "client satisfaction" feedback.

Project Cooperation

Lastly, cross-functional teams facilitate intro-project and inter-project cooperation. The very nature of a project calls for teamwork. Projects cannot be decomposed into discrete tasks assigned to individuals working in isolation. Project teams enabling cross-functional communication and cooperation also make possible -inter-project connections (Pinto and Pinto 1990: 208) providing for more strategic consistency in the firm's behavior and facilitating dissemination of "best practices."

Teamwork in Action

A study conducted jointly by Development Dimensions International (DDI), the Association for Quality and Partici pation (AQP), and *Industry Week* showed that 26% of the 862 surveyed executives used teamwork in at least some parts of their organization and that more than half of their workforce will be organized into self-managed teams within five years (Ju 1992; Wellins and George 1991). Another study of 277 firms from the *Fortune* Service 500 revealed that during 1960–1964, top level executive teams were managing only 8% of the companies surveyed; however, during 1980–1984, this percentage increased over threefold to 25 percent (Ancona and Nadler 1989: 19). The number of studies concerning teams and groups operating in the corporate setting, along with the publications devoted to team-based organization, clearly indicates that the popularity of teams is on the rise. They have become one of the favorite themes of management practitioners and scholars.

Impressive results lend credence to this fascination with groups and teams. For instance, it is believed that Japan as a nation is saving upwards of $5 billion per year as a result of the activities of one particular type of work groups: quality circles. By 1978, when quality circles had existed in Japan for sixteen years, total cumulative savings were estimated at $50 billion (Mohr and Mohr 1983: 19). To cite another example, Lawrence Bossidy, who until 1991 was vice chairman of General Electric, indicates that at GE Appliances alone, team-based organizational redesign decreased average annual inventory by $200 million.

Douglas Smith, a principal at McKinsey and Co., claims that a company applying new principles of organization based on teams and autonomous groups can cut its cost base by at least a third. The claim is based on results of companies that have already redesigned parts of their operations according to the new team-based "philosophy". An industrial goods manufacturer that cut costs and raised productivity by more than 50 percent and a financial services company which reduced costs by 34 percent are cited as examples (Stewart 1992: 93).

Evaluation

Promoters of the new principles of organization, such as J.R. Hackman (1990), strongly discourage the use of narrow monetary criteria in evaluating the performance of teams and groups. Instead, he suggests a three-dimensional evaluation of group effectiveness:

1. Output. The degree to which the group's output meets the standards of quantity, quality and timeliness of the people who receive, review and use the output.
2. Process. The degree to which the process of teamwork enhances the members' ability to cooperate in the future.
3. Experience. The degree to which the group experience promotes the growth and personal well-being of the team members (Hackman ed. 1990: 6).

Empirical research has demonstrated that well-managed teams produce impressive results in terms of productivity, member development and satisfaction (for example, Hackman and Oldham 1980; Hackman et al. 1975). Let us briefly examine an example of such teamwork in IBM, followed by a detailed discussion of two types of teams: top management cross-functional teams and middle management cross-functional teams. These two types of cross-functional teams appear to be crucial in gaining and maintaining a competitive advantage in the global marketplace.

CROSS-FUNCTIONAL TEAMS AT IBM[9]

In the mid 1980s, two senior consultants, Maurice Hardaker and Bryan Ward, set up and conducted a series of training sessions in *Process Quality Management* (PQM) with cross-functional teams at IBM. PQM is an action-oriented team process aimed at committing the entire management team to the task of improving business processes through careful identification of goals, activities critical to their achievement, and measures of success. As a result of the PQM sessions at IBM, changes were implemented through the manufacturing organization's work force, leading to better logistics and to the introduction of continuous-flow manufacturing in IBM's fifteen European plants. We shall consider the PQM process in some detail.

The two consultants started PQM by securing full commitment from the senior manager, in this case a vice president of manufacturing. Later in the process the consultants involved the senior manager's immediate team in the careful exploration of the task which involved the implementation of major changes in the materials-management process, including continuous-flow manufacturing. Next they focused on the implications of these changes on the company's manufacturing priorities. Key functional managers from various sectors of the company were invited to work on the projects critical for achieving the desired state. The group was limited to approximately twelve people so that the integration and coordination of the activities would not become unwieldy. The PQM sessions were generally not held in the firm's offices and were led by a neutral consultant.

3-Step Development Process

There are three steps to develop Process Quality Management:

1. collectively develop a clear understanding of the team's mission
2. identify the critical success factors for fulfilling the mission
3. identify core business processes and define how they relate to the critical success factors and fulfillment of the mission

I. Mission Development. The first step in developing a cross-functional teamwork process is collective development of a clear mission. Hardaker and Ward (1987: 113) stress that "if the mission statement is wrong, everything that follows will be wrong too, so getting a clear understanding is crucial. And agreeing on a mission may not be as easy as it may at first seem." There are three major obstacles to collective and clear mission development. First, managers from different parts of the organization usually concentrate on their separate functional missions. Second, managers' idea about the mission of an organization as a whole is usually vague. Third, the fact that management teams are composed of long-serving members and new arrivals, as well as of new leaders, makes finding a common language and interest difficult.

Collective missions at IBM were mutually constructed, publicly agreed upon, short, and precise. Hardaker and Ward (1987: 113) cite an example of such a mission in one of IBM Europe's units:

"Prepare IBM World Trade Europe Middle East Africa Corporation employees to establish their business."

"Organize high-level seminars for IBM customers and make a significant contribution to IBM's image in Europe."

"Demonstrate the added value of the International Education Centre through excellence in advanced education, internationalism, innovation, and cross-functional challenges."

This mission statement has a clear focus (to organize high-level seminars for IBM customers), sets explicit boundaries for the business (Europe, the Middle East, and Africa), and establishes measurable criteria of success (to demonstrate the added value of the center through excellence, internationalization, and so forth).

II. Goal-Setting. The second step of PQM is to explicate the goals of a business, business unit, or project that will work as the critical success factors (CSFs) for accomplishing the team's mission. Hardaker and Word (1987) clearly believe that effective teams can identify CSFs, while non-effective teams would not understand the implications of the mission statement for work in their unit. In the case of IBM, this postulate was proved by asking managers in 125 European companies to state their firm's five most critical success factors. Management teams of the most profitable companies agreed on 6 to 12 CSFs while executives of poor performers offered from 26 to 43 different statements (that is, they did not compose a team).

In order to develop manageable and clear CSFs consultants offer the following procedure:

1. Brainstorming. The team starts with a brainstorming session during which participants offer one-word descriptions of factors they believe could have an effect on the attainment of their mission.

2. Selecting. Using the necessary-and-sufficient rule, the team begins to restate the CSFs developed during the brainstorming sessions. Consensus must be reached that each CSF listed is a necessary factor for achieving the mission and that collectively they are sufficient to achieve the mission. Hardaker and Ward (1097: 114) comment, "This is a stringent requirement. The list of CSFs must

reflect the absolute minimum number of subgoals that have to be achieved for the team to accomplish its mission."

3. Finalizing. The list should contain both strategic and tactical factors in order to balance the long-term and short-term perspectives. The number of CSFs should not exceed eight because, in the consultants' opinion, eight is the largest number of critical goals that a team can manage well.

III. Identification of Key Processes. The third step of PQM is an identification of those business activities and processes that are vital to the mission statement, and takes into consideration as well the requirements imposed by critical success factors. Again a necessary-and-sufficient rule and the consensus of team members are necessary for developing a list of fundamental business processes. In order to make the list concise and accurate, Hardaker and Ward (1987: 114) recommended that the IBM teams take the following approach:

1. Each business process description should follow a verb-plus-object sequence

2. Each business process should have an "owner," meaning the person responsible for carrying out the process

3. The owner should be a member of the management team that agreed to the CSFs

4. No owner should manage more than three or four business processes

After establishing a list of core business processes, each of which is owned by one of the managers, the team must link the processes to the critical success factors in order to define those processes that are of utmost importance to the mission's success. The process starts with placing the processes and the CSFs in a random order on a matrix, as demonstrated in Figure 4.1. The team focuses on the first critical factor (best-of-breed product quality in Figure 4.1) and identifies those processes that chiefly influence the particular factor. Many, if not all, processes will impact each of the CSFs. However, the resources, attention, and time of managerial teams are limited. Therefore, a list of priorities to allocate time and money must be developed by ranking the processes. A two-tier procedure is employed.

First, the most important processes are identified as those intersecting the largest number of CSFs. Second, the team evaluates how well each process is currently being performed. As shown in Figure 4.1, teams at IBM used a subjective ranking based on the quality of the various processes as: A = excellent performance, B = good performance, C = fair performance, D = bad performance, and E = embryonic or not performed at all. Hardaker and Ward (1987: 118) comment on the matrix in Figure 4.1:

Figure 4.1

Turning a Mission into an Agenda

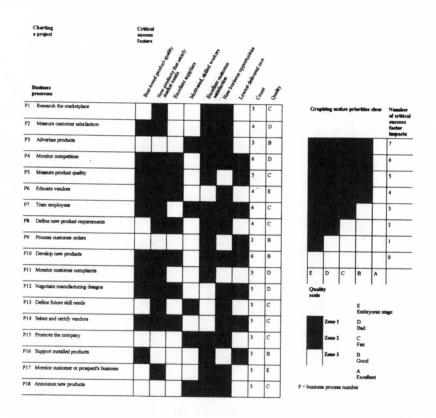

Source: Hardakar, M. and Ward, B. K. 1987. "How to Make Team Work." *Harvard Business Review*, November–December: 115

Graphing makes priorities clear...[T]he quality of each process is plotted horizontally and the number of CSFs the process impacts is plotted vertically. Then the team divides the graph into zones to create groups of processes. We can see immediately that Zone 1 contains the most critical processes. All the processes are important, by definition. But the higher risks (or higher opportunities) are found in Zone 1. These activities need the team's closest attention if the company is to improve market share and profitability within two years.

This matrix is a major input into the team's decision on how to allocate resources, establish relevant process measurements and controls, and implement necessary improvement-oriented projects throughout the organization.

Let us reiterate the conclusions drawn from the IBM example. Process Quality Management is but one strategy and set of tools for stimulating effective cross-functional teamwork. However, it illustrates the most important features of teamwork. A team must both achieve consensus on a clear mission and define CSFs. Brainstorming and other tools, discussed in the previous chapter, can be applied to stimulate the team's energy and creativity. A matrix of CSFs and business processes, along with a graph prioritizing the processes, is a useful tool for defining key business processes and then singling out those of critical importance. Finally, a team must follow through with an action plan that identifies resource allocation, improvements to be implemented, process measurements and controls, and a timetable. The team should conduct a periodic examination of the team's conclusions and action plan.

Let us now turn to a discussion of more general aspects of teamwork in two types of cross-functional teams: top management and middle management teams.

TOP MANAGEMENT CROSS-FUNCTIONAL TEAMS

Ancona and Nadler (1989: 22–23) find the following features characteristic of top management teams, which differentiate them from other types of teams, and provide for special group dynamics.

Salience of the External Environment. The key task of top management teams is to understand and manage organizations' relationships with the external environment. Several elements of that environment have a major impact on top management teams, particularly customers, competitors, suppliers, marketers, financial markets, and shareholders.

Complexity of the Task. Top management teams have to cope simultaneously with such tasks as strategic decision making, internal operations management, external relations management, institutional leadership, and so forth. All of these tasks are characterized by a high level of complexity and uncertainty.

Intensified Political Behavior. The essence of the role of a top management team is to exercise power within the organization, creating a uniquely political aspect.

Fixed Pie Rewards. While executive team members may be rewarded in many different ways, their ultimate reward is promotion to the position of CEO. The possibility of only one team member achieving the highest reward creates a zero-sum game.

Increased Visibility. Executive teams are highly visible and closely watched. They often become the subject of speculative gossip.

Composition. Ancona and Nadler found in the firms they studied that executive teams were composed of members with a strong need for power and achievement. Such ambitious individuals can make teamwork more difficult than for teams on lower levels.

Special Meaning of Team Membership. The importance of the top management in terms of its visibility, prestige and member rewards makes team membership especially desirable. Inclusion is perceived as a high reward and exclusion as a strong punishment. Managers are highly motivated to gain entrance and stay on the team.

Unique Role of the CEO as Team Leader. The CEO has final authority over team members. There is no one else to whom team members can appeal. The CEO cannot move up in the organization and usually retires from the position. Thus his tenure is potentially longer than in the case of other team leaders.

Teams in top management levels are still relatively new in the US. A vast majority of companies are still managed in a traditional way by a two-person CEO/COO structure. However, replacement of the COO by a team of managers is emerging as an alternative. Ancona and Nadler found teams acting in the COO position in

25% of companies they surveyed in 1984, as opposed to only 8% in 1964 (1989: 19). Three rationale were identified for the trend toward developing executive teams:

1. The need to respond to the complex and often changing external environment of the firm.
2. The need to manage highly diversified yet interdependent units inside the corporation.
3. The need to shape the process of executive succession to provide for increased stability and a wider range of candidates (Ancona and Nadler 1989).

Eisenstadt and Cohen (1990: 78–79) have studied the reasons for which organizations might turn to collective rather than individual leadership.

Reasons for Collective Leadership

Representative. The team's decisions are potentially more representative of the wide range of interests present in any organization, especially in a highly diversified multinational. Collective leadership enhances creativity due to the differentiated skills, perspectives and information resources of group members. Team members will likely better understand, support and implement organizational decisions which they helped to shape.

Communication. Communication among top managers is more efficient when they meet together regularly and work as a team. The job of managing is too vast to be accomplished by any single individual. Teams can spread the workload and ensure that all important matters are given adequate attention. Top management teams provide valuable opportunities for personal growth and development for their members.

Task Focus

Top management teams focus on four types of tasks:

1. Developing strategy for the organization as a whole as well as its key parts, ensuring consistency of the strategy.

2. Setting policies and rules.

3. Making operating decisions which are of key importance.

4. Developing the organization's architecture and its key human resources.

In order to accomplish these tasks executive teams are involved in three interdependent core processes: work management, external boundary management, and relationship management.

- Work management process relates to the way in which the team organizes and manages itself, shares information, sets the work agenda, makes decisions, coordinates activities, etc.

- External boundary management process determines how the company's boundaries are defined and how the key external actors are identified. In addition it focuses on identifying the key external actors (for example, governments, competitors, financiers) and determining the correct approach. The team must also manage its boundaries with other groups inside the organization.

- Relationship management process results in the degree of openness among members and the resolution of conflicts (Ancona and Nadler 1989: 24).

Teamwork on the top level of a giant multinational company can be exemplified by Asea Brown Boveri Ltd. (ABB).

ASEA Brown Boveri (ABB)

ABB is the world's largest industrial equipment producer, with revenues approaching $30 billion and nearly 215,000 people employed at its 1,100 companies and 4,500 profit centers operating in 140 countries. 31% of total ABB sales are made in EEC countries, 26% in EFTA countries, 21% in North America, 15% in Asia and Australia, and the final 7% in Africa, Eastern Europe, and Latin America (ABB 1991: 2–3).

ABB's worldwide business operations are organized into eight business segments: electrical power plants, electrical power distribution, electrical power transmission, industry systems, transportation systems, environmental control technologies, financial services, and a grouping of small diverse units. Each business segment oversees several business areas. ABB's strategy can be outlined as follows:

1. ABB assumes leadership in the core technologies used in all the business areas where it competes worldwide. Core technologies such as electronic control systems, diesel engines, computer software, combustion, and energy are used jointly by several business segments and dozens of business areas and are considered to be company resources. Cross-fertilization and international cooperation in R & D, product development and design are not only encouraged but planned and organized. Management teams are the main vehicle of such cooperation.

2. ABB operations are structured so as to enable economies of scale across country borders. ABB has factories highly specialized in components all over the world which are producing ten times the volume of its competitors. This specialization creates enormous cost and quality advantages over fragmented European competition. For example, in 1991 there were still 24 companies building locomotives in Western Europe, while the US and Japan had only two and three such companies respectively (Taylor 1991: 92–93). Managers of business segments and business areas, together with directors of the corporate research centers, are responsible for encouraging that degree of specialization in all of ABB's lines of business. This specialization is accomplished through a number of top management teams jointly focusing on the same problem from different perspectives.

3. When fulfilling orders from clients with a distinct nationality, ABB follows the principle of "think globally, act locally." An ABB company in that market, managed and staffed by local nationals, employing local engineers and workers, and registered on the local stock exchange put its name on such orders. Specially created teams of ABB engineers, designers, production managers, and service people work closely with the client during the design stage of the project and continue to do so during the manufacturing, installation, service, and development

stages. The top management teamwork principle is applied on the local level in the same way it is applied on the global scale.

Local top management teams make it possible for a global giant to adjust swiftly to local conditions and to offer in many countries "super local" services such as electrical installation that are completely determined by local regulations, technical infrastructure, and so forth (Taylor 1991).

A matrix structure is the backbone of ABB's organization. The business segments and areas make up the global side of the matrix. Managers responsible for business segments craft strategy, determine product mixes, allocate markets to different factories, and decide how factories should pool their expertise, research funds, and track engineering and managerial talents. They work with countless multinational teams of managers, experts and engineers and maintain a global perspective.

Country managers comprise the local side of the matrix. They stay close to the local market, cultivate client and government relations, negotiate with local trade unions, guarantee compliance with local laws and regulations, and assure that the company is perceived as local by its local customers, authorities and community. At the same time, however, they must understand and respect the company's global strategies and policies. Country managers participate actively in management teams of global reach involved in formulation of smaller or bigger pieces of global strategies and policies.

Access to "Abacus" (a highly sophisticated computerized reporting system) enables ABB's top management team, called the "executive committee," to constantly monitor major company developments. The executive committee is composed of thirteen members. Each is responsible for a business segment, a region, and some administrative function on the top management level. The executive committee meets for one day every three weeks in different locations to discuss key issues. The company headquarters in Zurich (Switzerland) is little more than a mail box and employs only about 100 people (Taylor 1991; Agthe 1990).

Few of the members of a truly multinational top management team are stationed in Zurich. For example, Eberhard von Koerber, member of the executive committee located in Manheim (Germany), is responsible for Germany, Austria, Italy, and Eastern Europe as well as for a worldwide business area: installation materials and some staff functions. Gerhard Schulmeyer, stationed in Stamford, Connecticut, is responsible for the North American region and the industry systems business segment. The business area leader for power transformers, who coordinates 25 factories in 16 countries, is a Swede named Sune Karlsson, vice president of ABB, who works out of Mannheim, Germany. The business area leader for instrumentation is British, the business area leader for electric metering is an American working out of North Carolina, and so forth (Taylor 1991).

In spite of the fact that only 30 percent of the ABB's managers are native English speakers, English is the official language of the company, which enables communication among different nationalities. The executive committee is a mixture of Swedes, Swiss, Germans, and Americans. Other management teams have even more complex nationality structures.

Such a small staff and management personnel is made possible by the informal "horizontal" management style practiced at ABB. As Agthe (1990: 41) states: "This type of management style substitutes collegiality and teamwork for hierarchical structure and it places the highest premium on entrepreneurial spirit." This management philosophy reduces the number of layers in management structures, increases the span of control through massive use of top management teams, and relies on personal competence, integrity, and superior leadership rather than on elaborate formal regulations, procedures, and so forth. ABB's managers are expected to provide strong leadership without being dictatorial. Their power and influence should be based on vision, competence, entrepreneurial spirit, and the ability to mobilize and motivate people by channeling their creativity toward common goals. In other words, they are expected to perform as both excellent team members and effective team leaders.

ABB's horizontal approach to management, that it, its heavy reliance on team organization, requires the exchange of an enormous amount of unstructured information. In addition to the use of Abacus as a structured information channel, unstructured information channels must flow between corporate levels and units, as well as between management teams operating on different levels. According to Barnevik, "you don't inform, you over-inform" (Taylor 1991: 104). This statement refers to the fact that the tendency to be selective about sharing information must be overcome. Common practices include working sessions and ad hoc team meetings composed of managers from around the world, who meet to discuss such practical topics as cutting cycle times, raising quality, or lowering accounts receivables. Such sessions take usually two or three days. Managers from different parts of the globe live in close quarters, communicate, discuss, design solutions, and meet with several members of the executive committee for an open dialogue. In this intensely interactive environment, cultural diversity is no longer a problem to overcome, but rather a valuable asset offering management teams a multi-focal perspective. Such a perspective is a key to success for a truly global enterprise.

Emergence of Top Management Teams

Top management teams may originate due to a number of factors. Three common scenarios are increasing business diversity, a new CEO, and the need to evaluate executive candidates. These scenarios are described below:

Business Diversity. The business diversity scenario is driven by the diversity and complexity of the business units forming a corporation. The scenario applies to companies in which the drive for diversification has created a complex multi-industry set of activities in an unstable multinational environment. These companies often experiment with unconventional organizational forms such as networks and collective forms of leadership (Miles and Snow 1986).

New CEO. This scenario concerns the appointment of the new CEO, who at first creates a team to help lead the corporation instead of immediately appointing a new COO. This delay in appointing a new COO may be due to a number of factors, including the CEO's desire to learn more about the organization, eliminate a layer in the company hierarchy, use the collective wisdom of a group, and assess the potential of different COO candidates. Using a management team in place of a COO may or may not become a permanent solution.

Executive Selection. This scenario occurs at the end of a CEO's term. In preparing for the appointment of a successor, the CEO may replace the current COO by a team composed of serious CEO candidates. The team then becomes a vehicle to evaluate the performance and potential of its members.

In companies where management teams are widely used on different levels, the three scenarios above may take place simultaneously.

MIDDLE MANAGEMENT
CROSS-FUNCTIONAL TEAMS

Middle management cross-functional teams result from a basic change called "core process redesign" or "process innovation." The main objective of such a change is to overcome the effects of physical barriers and constant "turf wars" between functional departments, as described above by "Palermo's Law." A new organizational structure is built around distinctive processes which can integrate the functions.

Process Management

Process innovation leads to process management by cross-functional teams. It differs from traditional management built around functions (such as production or marketing) in three ways:

- External measures. Process management uses external objectives and performance measures (such as inventory turnover) to show how the members are working as a team to keep costs low and sales high.
- Complementary skills. In process management employees with different skills are grouped together to accomplish a complete piece of work. For example, a mortgage loan officer, title searcher, and credit checker may work together as a team rather than moving files from one functional specialist to the next.
- Information flow. Information moves directly to where it is needed independent of the hierarchy. Employees request and receive information directly from the source without intermediaries and without asking supervisors for permission (Stewart 1992: 95).

Honda City

Cross functional teams develop on the middle management level to close the gap between the vague vision generated at the top management level and operational reality. In order to close this gap, cross-functional teams at the middle management level are given general and ambiguous instructions from upper management. For example, the team of designers that developed the Honda City car was given an overall assignment from headquarters to "create something different from the existing concept" (Nonaka 1988: 10).

The task guidelines are general, but the time constraints are made clear. With these instructions, a cross-functional team is free to choose not only its own mode of operation but also its own understanding of the general guidelines provided by the top management. In the case of Honda City, the innovative idea of a "horizontally long and vertically short car" (Nonaka 1988) was developed autonomously by the designing team.

Within the framework of middle management teams, functional specialists cooperate closely according to constantly changing patterns of tasks and corresponding information flows. In some companies special information systems are developed. The team which developed Honda City was composed of employees from the development, production, and sales departments. In order to facilitate cooperation among functional specialists with distinctively different skills, information sources, behavioral patterns, and the like, a special information system was created. "The system performed the following functions: procuring personnel, facilities and budget figures for the production plant; analyzing the automobile market and the competition and setting a market target and determining sale price and production quantity" (Nonaka, 1988: 11). The new information system enabled the team to immediately test new ideas.

Cross-functional teams must introduce, challenge, process, and integrate a wide range of information and ideas. At Honda, one of the methods used was *tamadasbi kai*. These were informal meetings held at different times and places to create and share information. For example a team developing Honda City often met in small taverns and restaurants for constant brainstorming. Attendance at such meetings was not strictly limited to team members. Quite often functional specialists from different, but related departments were also invited (Nonaka 1988).

Some organizers, such as producers of computers, software, industrial robots, and manufacturing systems, develop cross-functional teams to work closely with clients to jointly develop products. Quite often suppliers are also involved in cross-functional teams on the middle management level (Miles and Snow 1986; Reid 1990).

Constant information exchange with the top management plays an important role in cross-functional teams. However, because of the team's need for autonomy, this exchange is seldom used for purposes of traditional organizational management and control. Says Mr. Kawamoto, vice president in charge of R & D at Honda (Nonaka 1988: 11): "Basically speaking organizational management is no longer necessary if each individual properly performs what is expected. Once a goal is given and roles are specified to a certain extent, our staff works quite well."

Feedback from top management is mainly used to reject stock ideas and encourage creativity. Honda's top management is known for a strong tendency to repeatedly reject standard ideas which "looked like something else" and to even destroy its own accumulated knowledge in order to create something new and better. The Honda City car is undoubtedly innovative product. It was created by recreating both industry paradigms and Honda's own standard design. The engine, suspension and tires, as well as all other parts, were specially developed for Honda City. About ninety patents resulted from the project, clear evidence that new knowledge was cultivated (Nonaka 1988).

Innovation by Cross-Functional Teams

Peters (1991) makes a new "management fad" out of this obsession with innovation, calling it "violent market injection strategies." He advises (Peters, 1991: 10) the following: "Begin with the most radical strategies. In short: force the market into every nook and cranny of the firm. Let economist Joseph Schumpeter's powerful 'gales of creative destruction' not just refer to entrepreneurs attacking the establishment from the outside, but to a self-generating strategy for obsoleting ourselves

from the inside—before some outsider does it first." Self-obso-
leting strategies proposed by Peters include the following:
licensing the firm's most advanced technologies; cannibalizing
the most profitable products; selling or splitting off new units;
and selling off the old winners to force dependence on the new.

Cross-functional teams on the middle management level are
clearly the vehicle enabling top management to inject the
market into the firm. The loose structure and task orientation of
teams more easily allow for challenging existing paradigms and
for developing, testing, and implementing new ideas and
processes. Arthur D. Little's Deschamps and Nayak (1992: 46)
point out that cross-functional teams develop a clearer understanding of the customer, make better and more balanced
product decisions, react more quickly (provided they are given
autonomy), and have superior planning and coordination.

Information and Authority in Cross-Functional Teams

An empirical study of communication processes in 72 cross-
functional hospital project teams (Pinto and Pinto 1990) clearly
indicates that effective teams excel in their use of informal
communication and differ in the purpose of their communication. Better performing, highly cooperative teams exhibited a
high level of informal, unstructured communication. Effective
teams were likely to communicate during the brainstorming
process, obtain project-related information, review the development process, and receive feedback on their performance. The
study empirically confirms the linkage between project team
effectiveness, project performance (successful introduction of
new programs and services) and cooperation among managers
from different functional departments.

Information exchanged between top management teams
and cross-functional teams enable sound compromise between
centrally administered strategy and complete autonomy of the
middle management groups. However, lateral relationships
within and among cross-functional teams push more of the
strategic management down to the middle management layers
of the company. For example at ICI, a leading UK chemical
company, the authority of the company headquarters was
reduced so drastically that, as Chairman Denys Handerson
admits, his executive board has largely assumed the role of

communicators. Each member of the board monitors, through informal and unstructured contacts, a portfolio of company businesses. Says Handerson: "The directors are there primarily as a team to do things only they can do—and that is not second-guessing the leads at the next level" (Guterl 1989: 35). It is important to note that top management teams work *with* middle management cross-functional teams.

Cross-functional teams are also established to manage more structured processes than designing new car models introducing new programs and services. At Kodak, 1,500 employees, producing $2 billion a year of 7,000 different film products, work not in departments but in what is called "the flow." Twenty five teams watch the flow. Distinctive streams within the flow are defined by customers (such as health-care providers). Streams are monitored by customer-satisfaction measures (such as on-time delivery or number of customer complaints). Each stream is responsible for developing, manufacturing and selling its own products to its own clients. Within the streams, most employees work in self-managed teams. Only a few functions, such as accounting or human resources, remain centralized outside the streams. Kodak's black and white division, Zebra, saw drastic effects only two years after cross-functional teams implemented process innovation. The division's costs declined from 15 percent over budget to 15 percent under, its customer response time decreased from 42 to 21 days, and its record for late order fulfillment changed from 33 percent to 5 percent of total orders. Redesign of business processes and implementing cross functional teams also produced an increase in employee satisfaction. Organizing cross-functional teams around distinctive processes has become a new method of operation in many leading companies such as Hallmark, Xerox, and GE (Stewart, 1992).

Increasing numbers of multinationals are using top management and middle management cross-functional teams as a means to adopt "network-type" or "federation-type: organizational structures. The movement includes such global giants as IBM, Apple, Philips, and Digital Equipment Corporation. Replacing traditional hierarchical matrices with a network- or federation-based organization enables them to respond better to the challenges of competition.

CRITICAL SUCCESS FACTORS OF
CROSS-FUNCTIONAL TEAMS

Leading consulting firms, such as McKinsey & Co., offer assistance in corporate restructuring involving the dramatic replacement of the old traditional matrix by a network of cross-functional teams. The 10-point blueprint offered by McKinsey's Ostroff and Smith (1992) clearly outlines the issues addressed in this chapter:

1. Organize primarily around process, not task. Processes, rather than functional departments, should become the company's main building blocks.

2. Flatten the hierarchy by minimizing the subdivision of processes. Many parallel teams should be involved in complex multi-step processes.

3. Give senior leaders responsibility for processes and process performance.

4. Link performance objectives and the evaluation of all activities to customer satisfaction.

5. Make teams, not individuals, the focus of organization performance and design.

6. Combine managerial and nonmanagerial activities as often as possible.

7. Emphasize that each employee should develop several competencies. Few specialists are needed.

8. Inform and train people on a just-in-time "need to perform" basis, not on a "need to know" basis.

9. Maximize supplier and customer contact with everyone in the organization.

10. Reward individual skill development and team performance instead of individual performance alone.

These ten "new commandments" are very strongly against the culture of hierarchical corporations. Thus the following problems must be specifically addressed:

1. Choosing a Team Leader.   The team leader of middle management cross-functional teams is chosen by the top management. The Honda City project team was headed by Mr.

Hiroo Watanabe, a 35-year-old chief researcher. Mr. Kawamoto, vice president in charge of R & D, explained: "It's hard to get enough cooperation if you only have young staff members. Therefore I chose a skilled senior as their leader" (Nonaka 1988:10).

Barry (1991) indicates that the appointed team leader should allow for a heterogeneous "distributed leadership pattern." Enabling different people to take the initiative at different times involves performing the four basic leadership roles: envisioning, organizing, spanning, and advising. Cross-functional teams require quality leadership, although mistakes will likely be made and failures will sometimes occur. Recent management literature is full of descriptions of such failures resulting from leaders' inability to manage their cross-functional team (see Barry 1991; Hackman 1990).

It should be noted that a person's inability to manage one team effort does not exclude positive results when leading others. For example, the leader of one of the teams developing the F-16 jet fighter described his role as including the following responsibilities (Farr and Fischer 1992: 58):

- Defining the overall course and objectives of the program
- Designing policies for achieving these objectives
- Maintaining high motivation and morale for the people on the program team

The Metropolitan Life Insurance Company recommends that team leadership at the company be divided into two roles: developing client solutions and facilitating team operation (Denton 1992: 89).

2. Information Flow. Traditionally structured companies are often reluctant to make all information available to all employees. In fact, many corporate cultures include norms strongly opposing such principles. Royal Dutch Shell was quoted as an example of a company with open information flow when it implemented a sophisticated computerized management information system that enabled the unrestricted flow of information (Guterl 1989).

3. Rigid Career Tracks. Deeply entrenched functional career and promotion tracks and a habit of using narrow performance criteria are characteristics of traditional organizations.

Often promotion and even self-realization are closely related to climbing hierarchical ladders.

4. Reluctance to Share Information. Employees in hierarchical organizations are often reluctant to share their expertise and human talent with distant parts of the same organization.

5. Relations Among Departments/Divisions. Traditional organizations engender superficial, depersonalized relationships among members of the same organization. This problem is especially evident in relations between corporate headquarters and foreign subsidiaries. Management consultants working with a large US company to restructure the management of its Japanese subsidiary put it in the following way: "They [the American executives] didn't get out enough and play golf with the subsidiary executives. It is a typically American problem. The executive shows up at an eight o'clock board meeting and has to catch a plane for New York at noon" (Guterl 1989: 36).

6. Cultural Differences. Cultural differences abound among team members. After analyzing the cultural milieu of a project team, Philips & Goodman & Sackman (1992) identified the following types of cultural differences characterizing team members: geographically-based, societal-based (such as ethnic- or gender-based), cross-organizational (such as industry-based or professional), organizational, and sub-organizational (such as functional, hierarchical, project-based). In a complex environment, where people belong to many overlapping cultures, such impediments as negative stereotyping and difficulties with communication seem inevitable.

The most critical factor for the success of cross-functional teams, both on the top management and the middle management levels, is their placement within the proper framework of overall company strategies and structures. This general condition can be broken into the following elements:

- continuous improvement strategy with both a product and productivity focus
- network building
- development of core capabilities

Continuous Improvement Strategy. Continuous improvement strategies developed by teams are believed to have a greater chance of success. Compaq's CEO, Rod Canion, developed a strong preference for laptop computers, but his product creation team convinced him to give priority to a desktop PC based on the new 386 microprocessor. The decision was the right one because the market potential for the 386 was immense and the firm could not afford to develop both products simultaneously. The company respected the team's decision and was first on the market with its 386 PC. The success of the microprocessor enabled Compaq to skim the market and successfully complete the laptop project a few months later (Deschamps and Nayak 1992: 47).

Network Building. In order to achieve perfect coordination between product and productivity strategies, top management teams and the teams on the middle level are involved in product creation and development. Hewlett Packard is an example of a firm using teamwork to accelerate product creation and development processes. To implement the chairman's pledge to halve the break-even time on products, HP has developed a "tight project-team approach." Management uses a phased review process with well-defined milestones (milestone reviews). At Hewlett Packard, such reviews have three objectives (Deschamps and Nayak 1992: 48):

- to help the middle management team assess its performance
- to inform top management and consult with key decisions
- to resolve the issues that arise during a project's life cycle

Development of Core Capabilities. The development of core capabilities, describe by Leonard-Barton (1992: 112) as "differentiating a company strategically," is the principal job of top management teams. For example, at Apple Computers such core capabilities were identified as state of the art technology and design; a reputation for user-friendly, innovative products; a culture of risk taking and entrepreneurship; strong educational franchise and loyal customer base; brand awareness in all key markets, and creative advertising. Schoemaker (1992: 67) offers a four-step framework for developing a firm's core capabilities:

- generating broad scenarios of possible future situations
- performing a competitive analysis of the industry and its strategic segments

- analyzing the firm's and its competition's core capabilities
- developing a strategic vision

Such a strategic vision should be constantly updated as a result of the search for new core capabilities. Project managers, consciously using new projects as a vehicle for continuous improvement, constructively "discredit" traditional systems, skills, and values revered as the firm's core capabilities. In this way redefinition of the firm's traditional core capabilities and initiation of new core capabilities becomes possible (Clark and Fujimoto 1991).

This formidable task can be only accomplished by top management teams cooperating closely with the middle management teams. "Flexible facilitation, including techniques that encourage creative, nonlinear thinking is essential to successful application of this process in management teams. Usually follow-up staff work is indicated for the scenarios or competitive portions, and external consultants may be useful if limited in-house resources or expertise exist" (Schoemaker 1992: 80).

FIVE

International Benchmarking

Benchmarking is a process in which
companies target key improvement
areas within their firms, identify and
study best practices by others in these
areas, and implement new processes
and systems to enhance their own
productivity and quality. Many leading
companies are finding that in today's
globally competitive market, you
benchmark and improve—or you don't
survive. Benchmarking, a continuous
improvement process and partner of
the total quality movement (TQM),
enables companies to look outside
their own walls in the ongoing search
for excellence (Kendrick 1992:1)

Port et al. (1992:75) reports that 90% of the firms leading their
respective market segments in the Fortune International 500
survey attribute major portions of their competitive success to
benchmarking. However, several recent studies conducted in
Europe, Asia, and the Americas report that most firms do not
know how to effectively employ benchmarking practices to
enhance organizational quality and productivity (Kendrick
1992:1). In addition, many firms who attempt to utilize benchmarking practices invest lots of money and end up reducing
quality and productivity (Fuchburg 1992: 1). If benchmarking is
such an important tool for leading edge firms, and if at the same
time it is being so ineffectively employed by all except those

leading-edge firms, then it is imperative that we explore carefully its appropriate use. It will therefore be the purpose of this chapter to: (1) explore the appropriate focus, strategies, techniques, and research regarding the effective use of benchmarking; (2) investigate who the most effective benchmarkers are and how they proceed; and (3) isolate the critical success factors separating effective from ineffective benchmarking firms.

EFFECTIVE BENCHMARKING: FOCUS, STRATEGIES, TECHNIQUES, AND RESEARCH

> Benchmarking benefits as a strategic planning method are that it identifies the key to success for each area studied, provides specific quantitative targets to shoot for, creates an awareness of state-of-the-art approaches, and helps companies cultivate a culture where change, adaptation, and continuous improvement are actively sought out. (Altany 1990:14)

In one sense, benchmarking's rapidly increasing importance is a surprise to some managers. The process of benchmarking seems, on the surface, so straightforward and simple. A senior manager normally will start by deciding which part of an organization to benchmark. The manager then instructs the specialists in that area to map and begin collecting data on that process. Next, management locates a recognized world-class organization which excels in that same business process and offers to exchange information. After analyzing the data, a strategic plan is developed to incorporate the most effective approaches employed by the benchmarker firm. The simplicity of the process belies its true power and numerous pitfalls. In order to profit from the former and avoid the latter, we will explore benchmarking's (1) focus, strategies and techniques, and (2) the research available on its appropriate and inappropriate uses.

Benchmarking: Focus and Strategies

Most theorists distinguish three types of benchmarking: (1) strategic, (2) process, and (3) customer (Jenninga and Westfall 1992; Schmidt 1992; and Camp 1989).

Strategic. Strategic benchmarking compares the success of different companies to one another in creating long-term value for shareholders with that of industrial peers. This is accomplished by measuring such factors as total shareholder return on assets, the ratio of a company's market value to book value, the positive spread in a firm's return on capital and its cost of capital, and the value-added productivity per employee. Each of these measures provides some overall estimate of a firm's effectiveness in creating increased shareholder value given its general corporate strategy, and allows as well a comparison among similar firms that employ differing strategies. For example, Ernst and Young (*Business Week*, Nov. 10, 1992) classified over 500 firms as novice, journeymen, and master based on their respective return on assets (ROA) and value added per employee (VAE).

Firms classified as novice have an ROA under 2 percent and less than $47,000 VAE. Firms classified as journeyman had a 2–6.9 percent ROA and $47,000 to $73,999 VAE. Firms viewed as masters (Port et al. 1992:47), in other words those firms worthy of benchmarking, had a 7 percent or higher ROA and at least $74,000 VAE. Others argue that the premier firms in the world, or the top international strategic benchmarks, are best defined as those corporations which have earned more than their cost of capital every year for the past twenty years. Such a standard singles out only thirteen firms as valuable benchmarks. This select group includes American Home Products Corporation, General Electric, Philip Morris, and Rayathon from a wide range of industries (Schmidt 1992:8). In each of these cases, a firm is attempting to locate world-class benchmarks by employing some overall measure of an organization's strategic effectiveness as measured against the best competitors in the world.

Process. Process benchmarking, on the other hand, seeks to isolate one or more of a firm's primary business processes, for example, product development, billing and collection, integrated manufacturing, customer service, and then to benchmark that process against that of a world-class competitor with regard to process and product cost, quality and speed to market, and so forth. For example, Robert Camp, the manager of benchmarking competency at the Xerox Corporation, indicates that his firm operates in more than 100 countries and performs benchmarking in each. Over the past ten years, the list of firms against which Xerox has process-benchmarked has grown. Camp reports:

> It includes the names of some of America's largest corporations, including American Express Co. (billing and collection); American Hospital Supply Co. (automated inventory control); Ford Motor Co. (manufacturing floor layout); General Electric Co. (robotics); L.L. Bean, Hershey Foods Corp., and Mary Kay Cosmetics, Inc. (warehousing and distribution); Westinghouse Electric Corp. (National Quality Award application process, warehouse controls, and bar coding); and Florida Power and Light Co. (quality process). (Camp, 1992:3)

In addition, Xerox's Fugi, Japan facility won the 1980 Deming Award from the Japanese government for manufacturing quality. It therefore frequently employs internal benchmarking, whereby its manufacturing affiliates in Europe, the United States, and Africa benchmark their manufacturing practices against Xerox's affiliate in Japan. Both Xerox's top management and Robert Camp attribute Xerox's increased market shares and return to dominance in the photocopying field to the success of its international benchmarking of business processes (Camp 1989).

Customer.   Customer benchmarking involves surveying customers regarding what attributes they consider most important when purchasing the company's own product or that of its competitors. Then, given this attribute list, a firm benchmarks those attributes in competing firms' products in order to add them to their own product. Customer benchmarking entails the following four steps:

1. Identify the attributes that influence customer value perceptions.
2. Assess corporate performance.
3. Analyze competitors' performance and standing.
4. Close gaps between current performance and customer expectations.

For example, the Chrysler Corporation recently designed its new LH auto series by benchmarking the best attributes of other automobiles in the world. Chrysler took more than 200 dream attributes by customers of their ideal car and benchmarked them. They studied, among other attributes, the Acura Legend and Nissan Maxima for suspension systems, the BMW for ventilation and heating, and then designed a car with the best combination of these features available for its price range (Scarr 1992:A1). The emergent design is aimed at recapturing Chrysler's lost market shares in the mid-price range auto market. Customer benchmarking has been listed by such firms as Xerox, Motorola, and GM as a key strategy for regaining lost market share in their respective competitive markets.

Strategic, process and customer benchmarking against world-class competitors has become a major organizational tool for restoring firms to a position of excellence and increased stockholder value, business process excellence and market shares in the global marketplace.

Benchmarking Techniques

The actual processes involved in implementing a best practices program are varied. Xerox, one of the earliest firms to systematically employ benchmarking, employs a ten-step, four-stage process (see Figure 5.1).

Underlying this ten-step, four-stage process are several well-developed fundamental activities:

1. Know your own operation and carefully assess its strengths and weaknesses.

2. Locate world-class leaders and competitors to benchmark against.

3. Measure carefully productivity, quality and speed to market.

4. Analyze carefully how and why the benchmark is different from yours.

5. Incorporate and improve on the best practices to gain superiority.

Figure 5.1

The Benchmarking Process

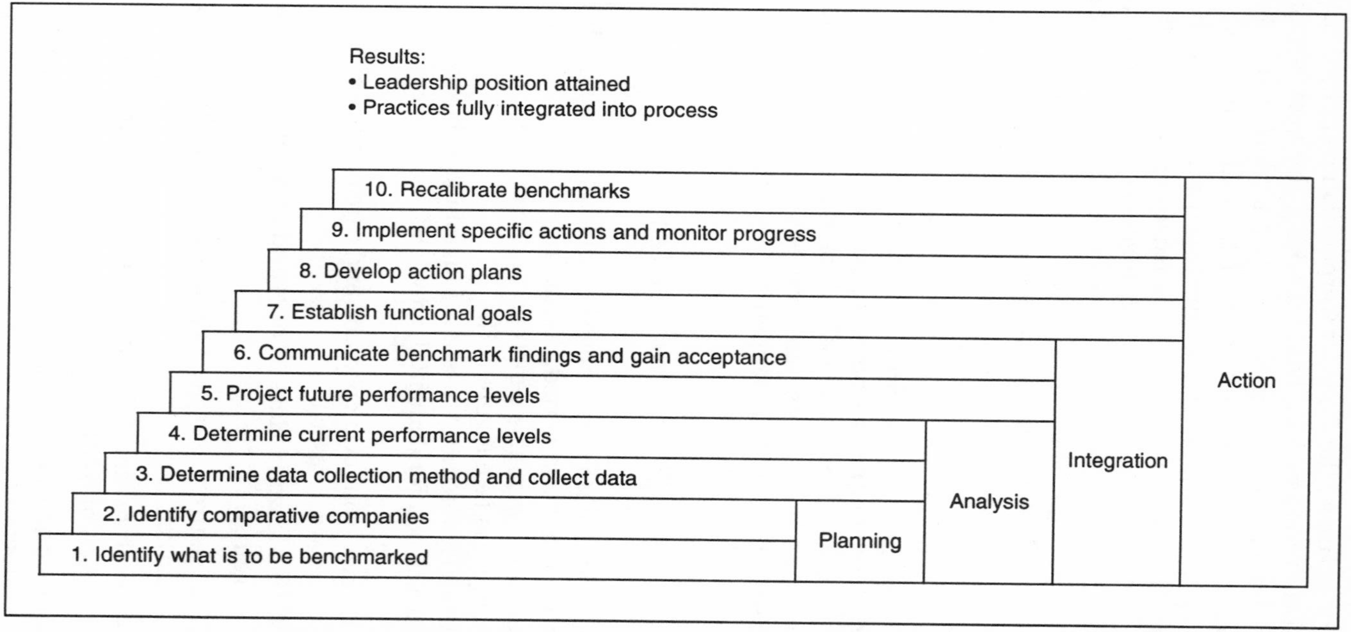

Results:
- Leadership position attained
- Practices fully integrated into process

10. Recalibrate benchmarks

9. Implement specific actions and monitor progress

8. Develop action plans

7. Establish functional goals

6. Communicate benchmark findings and gain acceptance

5. Project future performance levels

4. Determine current performance levels

3. Determine data collection method and collect data

2. Identify comparative companies

1. Identify what is to be benchmarked

Action

Integration

Analysis

Planning

Source: Camp, R. 1992. "Learning From the Best Leads to Superior Performance." *Journal of Business Strategy,* July: 4.

6. Continuously update benchmarking of your organization's central competitive processes.

7. Remember in the final analysis, the customer is the best judge of how good you are.

When unsuccessful, this benchmarking process normally fails at (1) the measurement phase, (2) the analysis of a different phase, and (3) in the cost of the benchmarking process given its benefits to the firm. For example, the International Benchmarking Clearinghouse surveyed over 80 companies and found that the average time and cost per benchmarking team per project was 878 hours per team member, that is, over 14 1/2 weeks per person with the full cost per project averaging $67,857. Given such a large up front investment, one must be careful to recover one's costs from one's efforts (Wiesender 1992:63).

Research Findings on the Appropriate Use of Benchmarking

In spite of the importance of benchmarking to organizational survival, recent studies reveal that most organizations cannot effectively employ organizational benchmarking to enhance their quality and productivity. The American Productivity and Quality Centers International Benchmarking Clearinghouse (IBC) surveyed 76 member organizations in 1992. The major findings included:

- Most firms (90 percent) consider benchmarking as a necessary tool for survival; however, most of the firms feel they don't know how to do it well.

- Eighty-three percent consider themselves beginner or novice users, with nearly half employing benchmarking less than two years.

- Only fifty percent have conducted 2–5 benchmarking studies. However, industry leading corporations had conducted 20 or more such studies, many on a regular basis.

- Leading companies in most industries are employing benchmarking effectively and 90% of those organizations also have other continuous improvement programs underway.

- Most important skills for benchmarking firms to master are process analysis, communication, and team functioning.
- Ninety percent report top management support, 80% use model steps, and 99% use team approach. (Kendrick 1992: 1).

Ernst and Young reported the results of a five-year study of over 500 firms on quality control. They concluded that only top performing firms have the internal skills, financial resources, and know-how to successfully benchmark the world's best firms. Table 5.1 summarizes their findings.

In short, the Ernst and Young study concludes that only master firms, that is, firms with an (ROA) of 7 percent and higher and a (VAE) of $74,000 and up have the skill, knowledge, and resources to measure, analyze, and implement superior business practices and only they can afford the $70,000 average cost for such benchmarking process.

WHO ARE THE MOST EFFECTIVE BENCHMARKERS AND WHY AND HOW DO THEY PROCEED?

A lot of companies are internally focused and just have not thought about going outside the company to get information...Some of these managers are locked into the mentality of improving only on last year's performance by 10%, and don't realize that another company might be 100% or even 1000% more efficient than they are in certain functions. By not identifying those areas and learning more efficient techniques, they remain behind. Company goals should always be geared towards being the best in the world, rather than just slightly better than last year.

—Jim Sierk, Vice Pres. of Quality at Xerox Corp. (Altany 1990:12)

If international benchmarking of world-class competitors is both essential to competitive success and very difficult to implement successfully (except for world-class competitors), how is a firm to proceed? Two issues arise which warrant our attention: (1) how do we learn how to be a world-class benchmarker, and (2) what firms and in what areas can and do we need to benchmark. Let us explore each of these issue in turn.

How Do We Learn to Be a World-Class Benchmarker?

Only recently have organizational practices begun to reveal a method for non–leading edge firms to develop world-class benchmarking capabilities. These practices involve the use of (1) internal benchmarking, (2) involvement in a benchmarking clearinghouse, and (3) competing for the Baldridge Award as progressive stages in developing world-class benchmarking skills.

Internal benchmarking. Experience teaches us that conducting internal benchmarking studies of several of one's own business processes can provide an inexpensive laboratory for the initial development of benchmarking skill. A firm begins by selecting a benchmarking team from the areas to be benchmarked and seeks outside consultants to train them in beginning benchmarking skills. The team then attempts to figure out how to measure, analyze, evaluate, and implement a best practices program between two or more functionally similar units of one's own firm. In addition, this is an excellent first step toward understanding one's own strategic, process, and customer processes. Such studies can be done in one-fifth the time and at one-fourth the cost of external benchmarking.

Involvement in a Benchmarking Clearinghouse. After several attempts at internal benchmarking, a firm should send its benchmarking teams to participate in the training and practice sessions of a benchmarking clearinghouse. Such clearinghouses provide intermediate training in benchmarking skills and an opportunity to study other non–leading edge firms. While the cost of such studies is slightly higher than internal benchmarking, the cost is less than competitive leading edge benchmarking. Several firms exist internationally to provide such services.

Table 5.1 How to Make Your Company a Quality Master

	NOVICE	JOURNEYMAN	MASTER
	Getting Started	Honing New Skills	Staying on Top
PROFITABILITY	Less than 2% return on assets (ROA)	2% to 6.9% ROA	ROA of 7% and higher
PRODUCTIVITY	Less than $47,000 value added per employee (VAE)	$47,000 to $73,999 VAE	VAE of $74,000 and up
EMPLOYEE INVOLVEMENT	$ Train heavily. Promote team-work, but forget self-managed teams, which take heavy preparation	$ Encourage employees at every level to find ways to do their jobs better – and to simplify core operations	$ Use self-managed, multi-skilled teams that focus on horizontal processes such as
	Limit employee empowerment to resolving customer complaints	Set up a separate quality-assurance staff	logistics and product development. Limit training, mainly to new hires
BENCHMARKING	Emulate competitors, not world-class companies	Imitate market leaders and selected world-class companies	$ Gauge product development, distribution, customer service vs. the world's best
NEW PRODUCTS	Rely mainly on customer input for ideas	Use customer input, formal market research, and internal ideas	Base on customer input, bench-marking, and internal R&D
SUPPLY MANAGEMENT	Choose suppliers mainly for price and reliability	Select suppliers by quality certification, then price	Choose suppliers mainly for their technology and quality

Table 5.1 *(continued)*

	NOVICE	JOURNEYMAN	MASTER
	Getting Started	Honing New Skills	Staying on Top
NEW TECHNOLOGY	Focus on its cost-reduction potential. Don't develop it – buy it	Find ways to use facilities more flexibly to turn out a wider variety of products or services	Use strategic partnerships to diversify manufacturing
MANAGER AND EMPLOYEE EVALUATION	Reward frontline workers for teamwork and quality	Base compensation for both workers and middle managers on contributions to teamwork and quality	Include senior managers in compensation schemes pegged to teamwork and quality
QUALITY PROGRESS	$ Concentrate on fundamentals. $ Identify processes that add value, simplify them, and move faster in response to customer and market demands. Don't bother using formal gauges of progress-gains will be apparent	$ Meticulously document gains $ and further refine practices to improve value added per employee, me to market, and customer satisfaction	Keep documenting gains and further refine practices to improve value added per employee, time to market, and customer satisfaction

Source: Port O. et al. 1992. Quality, *Business Week*, November 30, pp. 66–67.

Table 5.2 Scoring the 1991 Baldridge Award

1.0 Leadership (100 points)

    1.1   Senior executive leadership (40)
    1.2   Quality values (15)
    1.3   Management for quality (25)
    1.4   Public responsibility (20)

2.0 Information and Analysis (70 points)

    2.1   Scope and management of quaity data and information (20)
    2.2   Competitive comparisons and benchmarks (30)
    2.3   Analysis of quality data and information (20)

3.0 Strategic Quality Planning (60 points)

    3.1   Strategic quality planning process (35)
    3.2   quality goals and plans (35)

4.0 Human Resource Utilization (150 points)

    4.1   Human resource management (20)
    4.2   Employee involvement (40)
    4.3   Quality education and training (40)
    4.4   Employee recognition and performance measurement (25)
    4.5   Employee well-being and morale (25)

5.0 Quality Assurance of Product and Services (140 points)

    5.1   Design and introduction or quality products and services (35)
    5.2   Process quality control (20)
    5.3   Continuous improvement of processes (20)
    5.4   Quality assessment (15)
    5.5   Documentation (10)
    5.6   Business process and support service quality (20)
    5.7   Supplier quality (20)

6.0 Quality Results (180 points)

    6.1   Product and service quality results (90)
    6.2   Business process, operational, and support service quality results (50)
    6.3   Supplier quality results (40)

7.0 Customer Satisfaction (300 points)

    7.1   Determining custor requirements and expectations (30)
    7.2   Custor relationship management (50)
    7.3   Customer service standards (20)
    7.4   Commitment to customers (15)
    7.5   Complaint resolution for quality improvement (25)
    7.6   Determining customer satisfaction (20)
    7.7   Customer satisfaction results (70)
    7.8   Customer satisfaction comparison (70)

1,000 TOTAL POINTS

Competing for the Baldridge Award.   In the United States each year several quality awards are presented to leading edge firms. The national Baldridge Award is one such contest. Table 5.2. lists the scoring process for winning that award.

Preparing for competition in such a contest allows a firm to fine tune its overall performance at the strategic, process, and customer levels, competing against the nation's cutting-edge performers. This competition is an international world-class benchmarking experience. After one or two attempts at such an award, a firm normally enters the arena of world-class performers. Internal benchmarking, clearinghouse participation, and Baldridge Award competition is a five-to-ten-year climb into the arena of world-class benchmarkers. Past award winners have gone on to lead their respective market segments, develop world-class business processes, and become world leaders in strategic benchmarking.

What Firms and in What Areas Do We Benchmark?

Benchmarking is a tool for assessing the best practices of others and using the resulting stretch objectives as design criteria for upgrading one's own performance. Strategic benchmarking attempts to extend this process throughout an organization in order to achieve sustainable competitive advantage. Below are two lists of some world-class benchmarking candidates by business processes (Altany 1990:120).

The Creme de la Creme

Automated inventory control   Westinghouse
Apple Computer
Federal Express

Billing and collection   American Express
MCI

Customer service   Xerox
Nordstrom Inc.
L.L. Bean

Environmental management	3M Ben & Jerry's Dow Chemical
Health-care management	Coors Southern California Edison Allied Signal
Manufacturing operations management	Hewlett-Packard Corning Inc. Phillip Morris
Marketing	Helene Curtis The Limited Microsoft
Product development	Motorola Digital Equipment Sony 3M
Purchasing	Honda Motor Xerox NCR
Quality process	Westinghouse Florida Power & Light Xerox
Robotics	General Electric
Sales management	IBM Procter & Gamble Merck
Technology transfer	Square D 3M Dow Chemical
Training	Ford General Electric Polaroid
Warehousing and distribution	L.L. Bean Hershey Foods Mary Kay Cosmetics

Search and Employ

World-class benchmarking candidates (Altany 1991:15)

Benchmarking	Xerox
	Motorola
	Ford
	Florida Power & Light
	IBM/Rochester
	DEC
Billing and collection	American Express
	MCI
Customer focus	Xerox
	GE (plastics)
	Westinghouse
Design for manufacturing assembly	Motorola
	DEC
	NCR
Employee suggestions	Millikin
	Dow Chemical
	Toyota
Empowerment	Millikin
	Honda of America
Flexible manufacturing	Allen-Bradley/Milwaukee
	Motorola/Boynton Beach
	Baldor Electric
Industrial design	Black & Decker (household products)
	Braun
	Herman Miller
Leadership	GE: Jack Welch
	Hanover Insurance: Bill O'Brien
	Manco Inc.: Jack Kahl
Marketing	Proctor & Gamble
Quality process	Wallace Co.
	Florida Power & Light

	Toyota
	IBM/Rochester
Quick changeover	United Electric Controls
	Dana Corp./Minneapolis
	Johnson Controla/Milwaukee
R&D	AT&T
	Hewlett-Packard
	Shell Oil
Self-directed work team	Corning/SCC plant
	Physio Control
	Toledo Scale
Supplier management	Levi Strauss
	Motorola
	Xerox
	Ford
	3M
	Bose Corp.
Total productive maintenance	Tennessee Eastman
Training	Wallace Co.
	Square D
Waste minimization	3M
	Dow Chemical

Most of these world-class performers benchmark each other and regularly share benchmarking data. Some of these data are made available to clearinghouses and some are not. However, access to those world-class firms is restricted, unless you have something they want and are willing to share. Let us explore one attempt at such a sharing process between a large world-class Japanese firm and a small American firm.

The Danville, Illinois, Bumper Works

In 1978, Mr. Shahid Khan, a naturalized U.S. citizen from Pakistan, borrowed $50,999 from the Small Business Loan Corporation and took $16,000 of his own savings to establish the 100-employee Bumper Works in Danville, Illinois. This company designed and manufactured truck bumpers. Between 1980 and 1985, Mr. Khan approached the Toyota Motors Corporation on several occasions, attempting to become a supplier of bumpers for their trucks, but without much success.

In 1987, the Toyota Motors Company called together a group of 100 potential suppliers and released their design, quality, quantity, and price-range specifications for the product. The officials at Toyota Motors also indicated that they expected increased quality and a reduction in price each year from the supplier. By 1988, only Mr. Khan's Bumper Works company could produce a product which met Toyota Motors' exacting requirements.

In 1989, Toyota Motors sent a manufacturing team to Danville, Illinois to negotiate the contract and coalignment agreement between the two firms. The negotiations failed because the Bumper Works could not produce 20 different-sized bumpers and ship them in a single day. If Bumper Works could not do this, Toyota's truck production would slow down, because a single batch production line was used for all Toyota trucks. The truck price would increase dramatically (White 1991:A7).

Mr. Khan called a "town meeting" of workers from his own and Toyota Motor's Japanese factories to explore how this problem might be solved within Toyota's design, quality, quantity, and price requirements. It was decided that Bumper Works would have to switch the factory from a mass production to a batch production line and that a massive stamping machine, which required 90 minutes of manpower to change each cutting die, would have to be modified so that changes could be made in 20 minutes (White 1991:A7).

Next, the workers at both Bumper Works and Toyota Motors set up cross-functional teams to make a process map of current production procedures. They studied, simplified, and restructured the process to allow for batch production. The large stamping machine was studied for modifications that would speed up die changes. All this was done with considerable help from Toyota Motors, which had solved these same problems, but in a different way, back in Japan (White 1991:A7).

At this point, the Bumper Works' remodeled assembly line was ready to begin production. For six months, employees with stopwatches and cost sheets observed the restructured process and benchmarked its operations against the world-class standards of the Toyota Plant in Japan, but they still could not meet Toyota's quality, quantity, and speed of delivery specifications. They videotaped the process, studied it, and sent it to Japan for review. In July, 1990, Toyota Motors sent a team over to help retrain the workers. They returned again in December of 1990 to fine-tune the process and so meet Toyota Motors' contract requirements.

The new production line increased productivity over 60 percent above the previous year, decreased defects 80 percent, cut delivery time by 850 percent, and cut waste materials cost by 50 percent. A manual and videotape of the manufacturing process, the first of their kind at Bumper Works, were prepared for training. In addition, continuous improvement teams were formed in order to meet Toyota Motors' contract requirements for increased quality and decreased costs.

The representatives of each unit involved in the value chain linking Bumper Works and Toyota Motors had communicated their interests, concerns, and contributions to the coalignment process. Each firm's management, therefore, was able to forge a linking process that was satisfactory and optimizing to the value-added activities of each organization, creating a sustainable competitive advantage. Mr. Khan, the owner of Bumper Works, has profited from this experience and is building a new plant which will employ 200 workers in Indiana and will supply truck bumpers for a new Isuzu Motors plant located there (White 1991:A7).

CRITICAL SUCCESS FACTORS FOR INTERNATIONAL BENCHMARKING

The Japanese word *dantotsu* means striving to be the best of the best. It captures the essence of benchmarking, which is a positive, proactive process designed to change operations in a structured fashion to achieve superior performance. The purpose of benchmarking is to increase the probability of success of an attempt to gain a competitive advantage. (Camp 1992:3)

World-class benchmarking is an essential tool used by cutting-edge firms, one that is difficult to acquire the appropriate skills to employ. However, once the skills have been developed and employed, they are what separate world-class performers from also-runs. The acquisition and development of such skills normally follow a three-stage necessary acquisition process:

1. internal benchmarking
2. clearinghouse participation
3. competitive participation in The Baldrich Award.

This three-stage process involves practice in three types of benchmarking with world-class competitors:

1. strategic
2. process
3. customer benchmarking.

These three types of benchmarking all employ a four-stage process:

1. planning
2. analysis
3. integration
4. action.

In all of these stages, successful benchmarking depends on the appropriate measurement, analysis, and implementation of other firms' best practices.

SIX

Developing Strategic Linkages

> There is currently a convergence of
> attention and concern among man-
> agers and management scholars
> across the basic issues of organiza-
> tional success and failure...Successful
> organizations achieve strategic fit with
> their environment and support their
> strategies with appropriately designed
> structures and management pro-
> cesses, less successful organizational
> typically exhibit poor fit externally
> and/or internally. (Miles and Snow
> 1989: 10–11)

A rationale is provided for these claims based upon four distinctions, all of which characterize an organization's capacity to
negotiate an appropriate linking strategy with its customers,
and then order its organizational structures and processes in a
strategic manner.

Minimal fit among strategy, structure, and process is
essential to all organizations operating in competitive
environments. If a misfit occurs for a prolonged period,
the result usually is failure.

Tight fit, both internally and externally, is associated
with sustained, excellent performance and a strong
corporate culture.

Early fit, the discovery and articulation of a new pattern
of strategy, structure, and process, frequently results in
performance records which in sporting circles would

merit Hall of Fame status. The invention or early application of a new organization form may provide a more
powerful competitive advantage than a market or technological breakthrough.
Fragile fit involves vulnerability to both shifting external
conditions and to inadvertent internal unravelling. Even
Hall of Fame organizations may become victims of dete-
riorating fit. (Miles and Snow 1989: 10–11)

Successful organizational coalignment or fit is both a state
and a process. In practical terms, the basic alignment mecha-
nism is some communication strategy for coaligning the various
parts of an organization's value chain in a manner that takes
advantage of competitors' weaknesses while forming a tight fit
with one's customers. However, since competitors tend to learn
quickly from their mistakes and adjust, organizational coalignment activities are an ongoing process of continuously
improving an organization's fit with its environment in a way
that sustains its competitive advantage.

Chapter 1 argued that all organizations attempt to obtain
competitive advantage in one or more of the following ways: low-
cost products, product differentiation, product scope, and speed
to market. However, quick market saturation, shortened product
life cycle, and unexpected competition are creating a volatile
business climate that forces firms to adjust simultaneously to
change and to pursue all of these sources of competitive advantage. This volatile organizational environment consists of
customers with specific concerns and needs and of competitors
with products based upon their unique strategic response to
such customer concerns and needs. Further, it was argued that
once an organization scans the environment and notices a
change, then the firm's management must examine its own
configuration and settle upon a strategy for focusing its internal-
external resources into a pattern of linkages or capabilities in an
effort to create and/or maintain a competitive advantage.

Chapter 2 argued that once an organization understands
the concerns and needs of its customers, the coalignment
strategies pursued by its competitors, as well as the type of environment in which its products will compete (mature, export,
import, declining, emerging, and so forth), and explores the
internal and external resources available in its value chain for
generating organizational capabilities that can develop a

competitive advantage, then and only then can a firm's continuous improvement programs be focused so as to fine-tune the firm's linking activities in a way that achieves a sustainable competitive advantage. An organization's continuous improvement program includes the theoretic functions of negotiated linkages, aimed at improving organizational coalignment; self-managed teams, aimed at improving an organization within units linkages; cross-functional teams, aimed at improving an organization between unit linkages; international benchmarking, aimed at imitating a world class pattern of linkages employed by other firms; and organizational breakthroughs, aimed at generating new world class organizational capabilities. Finally, we explored in some detail the strengths and weaknesses of three specific models of continuous improvement programs: Quality Circles, TQM, and Work-Out. Chapters 3 and 4 discussed self-managed and cross-functional teams in detail.

The bottom-line claim of the first two chapters was than an appropriate use of continuous improvement programs requires a strategic theory of negotiated linkages as a prerequisite for its effective and systematic use. Such a theory would guide an organization effort in establishing a pattern of organizational capabilities which can serve as a source of sustainable competitive advantage. Up until now little attention has been paid to explicating these important strategic and theoretic process. It will be the purpose of this chapter to explicate and illustrate such a strategic theory. More specifically, we will (1) analyze organizational linking or coalignment process; (2) explore one strategic and theoretic perspective for creating a pattern of linkages or organizational capabilities for generating a sustainable competitive advantage; and (3) outline the critical success factors involved in this process. Let us address each of these issues in turn.

OUTSIDE LINKING TEAMS

In recent years there has been a move away from spreading conglomerates based on hierarchical structures towards more focused, flexible firms based on network structures of organization. The 1970s strategy of risk spreading by being big and diverse is giving way to the strategy of being focused and flexible in the 1990s - by subcontracting, engaging in joint ventures, and disentangling conglomerate divisions to function as entities within themselves. (Barnett and Wong 1992: 12)

In 1989, the Center for Information Systems Research at the MIT Sloan School of Management argued that an organization's ability to continuously improve effectiveness in managing its external and internal organizational linkages was the central element in successfully responding to competitive forces operating in the 1990s (Rockart and Schort 1989). Effectiveness in managing an organization's external and internal linkages refers to an organization's ability to achieve *coalignment* among its internal and external resources in a manner which is equal to or greater than existing world class benchmarks. In order to understand this coalignment process we will (1) conceptualize the coalignment process; (2) explore an organization's value chain as the central structure and processes requiring coalignment; and (3) briefly review the literature regulating the coalignment process.

Conceptualizing Coalignment

Coalignment is a unique form of organizational interdependence in which each of the units or elements in a firm's value chain clearly articulates their (1) needs, (2) concerns, and (3) potential contributions to an organization's functioning, in such a manner that management can utilize this information to forge an appropriate, value-added configuration and sustainable competitive advantage to the linkages. An appropriate value-added pattern of linkages between units is one in which management can integrate, coordinate, and control each unit's needs, concerns and contributions so that the outcome is mutually satisfying to the units involved and optimizing in value added activities of the organization as a whole.

World-class benchmarking refers to the standards or targets set for improving organizational performance. These benchmarks or goals, aimed at improving an organization's ability to respond to environmental change, must be set at a world-class level if one is to compete with or go beyond world-class standards, if one is to establish a sustainable competitive advantage. Only then will improvements in an organization's external and internal linkages or coalignment process provide the value-added gains necessary for sustainable competitive advantage.

The Value Chain Theory as the Organizational Structure and Processes Requiring Coalignment

All the organizational activities involved in delivering a product to its customers can be represented visually as a set of linked functional units and/or business processes, that is, as an organization's value chain (see Figure 6.1 below).

As you examine an organization's functional units level of the value chain, notice that the two circles denoting suppliers and customers are normally found *outside* the organizational structure, while the square boxes denote functional activities performed *within* an organization's structure. In examining an organization's business process level, note how each process includes some functional units unique to each business process and some that overlap with other business processes.

Figure 6.1

An Organization's Value Chain

Functional Business Unit Level

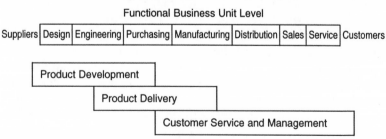

Note: Revised from Rockart & Short, 1989: 1

In order to understand where the source or sources of a firm's competitive advantage come from and how each organization's functional units and business processes add value or fail to add value to products, we must analyze an organization's value chain.

In addition, we need to benchmark each of these functional units and business processes to see if they provide a basis for a sustainable competitive advantage. In analyzing an organization's value chain, it is of paramount importance that those functional units and business processes are linked or coaligned so that value-added activities gained in one functional unit or business process are not lost due to the poor performance of other functional unit or business process. From a management perspective, the particular configuration of an organization's value chain and its coalignment linkages create several very specific problems.

First, it is important to understand that in different types of markets (that is, mature, export, service, declining, and so forth), the continuous improvement of some functional unit and/or business processes are more important to maintaining or gaining market shares, while others are less important or not important at all (Venkatraman and Prescott 1990).

Second, it may be the case that due to certain external linking activities such as joint ventures, technical alliances, or outsourcing, certain parts of the value chain reside partially or wholly within other organizations. However, the contribution of the other organization's value-added activity to our firm's value chain can only be realized when the two organizations are appropriately coaligned. Thus, the effective use of continuous improvement programs to coalign these value-added activities resides in other firms or between the two firms. If many such linkages exist, or if only a few exist but they are critical to the product's performance, then control of the value chain will reside outside the firm. In all cases, appropriate monitoring and control processes must be established (Kanter 1989).

Third, the functional units and/or business processes of a firm's value chain may be located anywhere on the globe where value-added activity or competitive advantage may be gained; however, continuous improvement programs must transcend these geographic distances if the value-added activities of each unit or business process are to be realized. For example, *product development processes* of the value chain are normally located in regions where firms have access to a steady supply of state-of-the-art engineers, as in Japan, the United States, and Germany, where competitive advantage can be obtained from product differentiation. *Product delivery processes* normally are located near sources of inexpensive skilled labor, as in the case of production facilities in Mexico, Spain, China, and Singapore, where competitive advantage comes from low-cost production. *Customer service* is normally located in the core markets where the customers reside in order to obtain competitive advantage from the ease and speed of services. The coalignment and continuous improvement of these geographically distant processes must be established, monitored, and improved through telecommunication processes. In such cases, coalignment will depend on the communication and information technology needed to track organizational activities in real time (King and Cushman 1993).

The Literature Regulating Coalignment Processes

Several empirical studies have been conducted which indicate that appropriate coalignment (1) is a unique source of competitive advantage; (2) varies by types of product markets; (3) may depend upon the coordination of strategy between organizations; (4) can separate successful from unsuccessful multinational organizations; and (5) depends upon the continuous improvement of critical organizational linkages to remain successful.

Powell (1992) undertook a study of organizational coalignment and competitive advantage in 250 firms located in two manufacturing industries. The data revealed that "some organizational alignments do produce supernormal profits independent of the profits produced by traditional industry and strategy variables" (Powell 1992: 121). The author concluded that the "concept of competitive advantage need not be confined to traditional economic variables, but may be extended to such nontraditional variables as organizational alignment" (Powell 1992: 129).

Venkatramen and Prescott (1990) undertook a study of the improvement of various organizational functions and processes and their effect upon market shares and return on investment (ROI) in seven types of markets. They classified markets into export, stable, fragmented, service, emerging, mature, and declining. Employing a sample of 821 firms across a variety of industries, they tracked their continuous improvement processes at two points in time, from 1976 to 1979 and from 1980 to 1983. Their results indicate that, depending on the type of market, some improvements in organizational functions or processes had a positive effect on market share and ROI while others had a negative effect. For example, in a mature market, investment intensity and increase in relative direct costs that resulted from continuous improvement programs had a negative effect, accounting for 80% of the variance in a decline in ROI and 20% of the variance in a decline in market share. Conversely, a decline in compensation for workers relative to the industry and a decline in prices increased both market share and ROI. This research program suggests that continuous improvement programs must target the appropriate organizational functions and business processes in different types of environments or suffer negative economic consequences.

We have already discussed in the former chapter the Nohria and Garcia-Pont (1991) study of auto firms, where portions of their value chain resided in another organization due to external linking agreements such as joint ventures, alliances, minority holdings, and so forth. In the process of exploring such linkages in the global auto industry, these authors found that between 1980 and 1990 the appropriate coalignment of such strategic blocs of firms contributed significantly to the competitive advantage obtained by the focal firm. However, the lack of strategic coalignment led to the loss of market shares (Nohria and Garcia-Pont 1991: 105).

Cvar (1986) attempted to determine if the rapid coalignment of a firm's internal and external sources relative to one's competitors could separate successful from unsuccessful firms in a volatile environment. Twelve industrial corporations were studied, eight successful and four unsuccessful firms across industries. Four of the successful firms were American and the remaining four were, respectively, Swiss, British, Italian, and French. Three of the four unsuccessful firms were American and one was Swiss. Successful firms were distinguished from unsuccessful by their high investment in coalignment processes, which allowed a quick response to environmental changes.

Smith, Grim, Chen, and Garnnon (1989) questioned 22 top managers from high technology firms. These researchers explained major portions of the variance in organizational performance, increased profits, and increased sales from coalignment processes. They found that an external orientation, a rapid responses to competitor products, and the radicalness of the change initiated in an organization's coalignment were related to increases in organizational performance.

Our brief summary of the empirical literature has led to some significant generalizations about the continuous improvement of organizational linking or coalignment processes. This research suggests that appropriate coalignment is (1) a unique source of competitive advantage; (2) varies positively and negatively by specific organizational functions and processes in different types of product markets; (3) may depend upon the coalignment of aspects of the value chain residing in other corporations; (4) can separate successful from unsuccessful firms; and (5) requires continuous improvement of critical organizational linkages to remain successful. Attention is now directed to the strategic perspective governing these coalignment or linking processes.

ONE STRATEGIC AND THEORETIC PERSPECTIVE GOVERNING COALIGNMENT OR LINKAGING PROCESSES

In theory network forms allow large organizations to exist without encumbered inefficiencies of over-burdened line structures. It is worth noting, however, that network conglomerates have become feasible only in the past few years due to advances in information technologies. Thus, organizations, for the first time, have the opportunity for more dynamic horizontal and structural communication linkages. Quite possibly, only those conglomerates that utilize these new structural and communication mediums can and will survive. (Barnett and Wong 1992: 12)

From both a theoretic and a strategic perspective, the management of appropriate organizational linkages aimed at creating a strategic capability, which will yield a sustainable competitive advantage, is the key to organizational success in the 1990s. Attention is now directed to an explication of this key theoretic and strategic process. More specifically, we shall: (1) explore the process of environmental scanning in order to locate potential sources and strategies for obtaining competitive advantage; and (2) explicate a theory for converting value chain potential into strategic organizational capabilities which when linked to customers will create sustainable competitive advantage. Let us explore each of these in turn.

The Process of Environmental Scanning

According to Preble, Rau, and Reichel (1988: 5) environmental scanning involves "that part of the strategic planning process in which emerging trends, changes, and issues are regularly monitored and evaluated as to their likely impact on corporate decision making." Environmental scanning usually entails (1) gathering data, (2) analyzing data, and (3) selecting a strategy.

Gathering Data.   Gathering data involves partitioning the external environment into meaningful sectors such as the industry environment, the competitive environment, and the general environment. The industry environment data normally is tracked in three areas: product information, market information, and customer information. Product information is scanned in four areas: products covered in the industry, the current state of each product, range of products developed recently, and technological advancement in products. Market information is gathered in three areas: a list of markets covered in the industry, the condition of each market (emerging, saturated, and so forth), and total share of market covered already. Customer information is gathered in three areas: identification of customers and their needs, changes in their needs and habits, and geographic distribution and habits of customers. The competitive environment data is normally collected in three areas: a list of the most threatening competitors and their market share trends and sales strategies, their technological and R&D capabilities related to competitive advantage, and their financial, technological, and managerial resources. The general environment data is normally collected in four areas: economic information, government plans and policies, supplier information, and manpower information.

Monitoring an organization's industrial, competitive, and general environment is useful only if this information is analyzed and utilized judicially.

Analyzing the Data.   Analyzing the data obtained in environmental scanning is both a simple and complex process. It is simple in that the critical information required to analyze the underlying dynamics of an industry and market are frequently readily available from all the competitors. It is complex in that the number of areas monitored to affect this dynamic may be large. Let us explore the elements in the process via a concrete example.

Jack Welsh, CEO of General Electric, a very successful global competitor, describes the two levels of environmental scanning and their effect on corporate alignment within his firm. Once a year, at the annual meeting of GE's top 100 executives, each of the firm's 14 business leaders is required to present an environmental scanning analysis of his or her respective business. Each business leader is asked to present one-page answers to five questions (Titchy and Charzon 1989: 115):

1. What are your business global market dynamics today and where are they going over the next several years?
2. What actions have your competitors taken in the last three years to upset those global dynamics?
3. What have you done in the last three years to affect those dynamics?
4. What are the most dangerous things your competitors could do in the next three years to upset those dynamics?
5. What are the most effective things you could do to bring about your desired impact on those dynamics?

Welsh concludes:

Five simple charts. After those initial reviews, which we update regularly, we could assume that everyone at the top knew the plays and had the same playbook. It doesn't take a genius. So when Larry Bossidy is with a potential partner in Europe, or I'm with a company in the Far East, we're always there with a competitive understanding based on our playbooks. We know exactly what makes sense; we don't need a big staff to do endless analysis. That means we should be able to act with speed. Probably the most important thing we promise our business leaders is fast action. Their job is to create and grow new global businesses. Our job in the executive office is to facilitate, to go out and negotiate a deal, to make the acquisition, or get our businesses the partners they need. When our business leaders call,, they don't expect studies, they expect answers. Take the deal with Thomson, where we swapped our consumer electronics business for their medical equipment business. We were presented with an opportunity, a great solution to a serious strategic problem and we were able to act quickly. We didn't need to go back to headquarters for a strategic analysis and a bunch of reports. Conceptually, it took us about 30 minutes to decide that deal made sense and then maybe two hours with the Thomson people to work out the basic terms. (Tichy & Charzon, 1989, p. 115).

Environmental scanning allows us to focus on the forces external to an organization that significantly influence its internal relationships.

Selecting a Strategy. The strategy should be based upon a careful analysis of one's environment. A careful analysis of one's competitors involves exploring each link in a competitor's value chain to see which, if any, functional units and/or business processes might be a potential source of competitive advantage for either one's competitors or one's self. Once this process has been repeated for each of the most threatening competitors, then a firm can prepare a strategic outline of potential sources of competitive advantage for the industry. As soon as this outline is complete, a firm is in a position to select a strategy for dealing with each of its competitors. Five such strategies appear evident: (1) confront, (2) focus, (3) circumvent, (4) join, and (5) withdraw.

Confront. When a value chain comparison reveals substantial competitive advantage at both the functional and business process level of competition, then a firm can undertake head-to-head confrontation. Toyota chose to confront

Mercedes and BMW in the U.S. luxury car market with its Lexus car, because Toyota believed it could obtain sustainable competitive advantage in price from each of its functions and business processes, while generating quality equal to or greater than that of its two competitors. The results were dramatic. Toyota grabbed 23 percent of the market, all at the expense of Mercedes and BMW, while ranking lowest in customer complaints (47 per 1000 cars), while Mercedes had 99 per 100 and BMW 141 per 100 (USA Today, June 3, 1991: B3).

Focus.   When a value chain comparison reveals an insignificant competitive advantage at both the functional and business processes level except in one area of important concern to the customer, then one can focus upon manifesting a competitive advantage in that area. VISA Credit Card company developed an artificial intelligence system for electronically approving credit card purchases within sixty seconds. This electronic system cut down the average store owner's nonpayment of purchase slips by 82% per year. This saves both VISA and the stores it services billions of U.S. dollars per year. By focusing on this aspect of its value chain, VISA has dramatically increased its market share while decreasing its bad debts (Feigenbaum, McCorduck, and Ni 1988).

Circumvent.   When a value chain comparisons reveals a substantial competitive advantage from circumventing some aspect of a competitor's value chain, then a firm can undertake head-to-head competition. For example, Parrigo is a private drug firm which manufactures any liquid, pill or capsula which is a large seller and which is off patent. It contacts major sales outlets and produces a product in the same size, shape colored package and content as a well-known brand product. However, where the brand name would normally appear, it places the name of the chain store selling the product. Since Parrigo has no R&D costs and no advertising costs, it can market its products at a much lower cost than its competitors can. When the product is put on a chain store shelf, near to the brand product, most customers can't tell the difference in package and content. The customer thus picks up the less expensive product, which offers large savings to the customer, as well as larger profits to the chain and Parrigo then does its brand name competitors. By circumventing the R&D and advertising elements of its competitors' value chain, Parrigo creates a sustainable competitive advantage.

Join. When a value chain comparison reveals a substantial competitive advantage for your competitors, either for some aspect of their product or for all of their product, then one can form whatever type of alliance is appropriate to obtain the use of that aspect or product. General Motors found that the Japanese automakers could produce a compact car at $500 per car less than GM could. GM then formed a joint venture with Toyota and Mitsubishi to produce and sell cars under the GEO brand name. Today the GEO series of cars, one of GM's largest-selling auto segments, is produced in that manner because GM joined with Toyota and Mitsubishi in a negotiated linking arrangement.

Withdraw. When a value chain comparison reveals a substantial competitive advantage for your competitor for some aspect of a product or the total product, when that competitor will not join you in any way and you cannot circumvent the aspect or product, then a firm may withdraw its product from the market in order to preserve its own reputation for other products in the market. This withdrawal may be temporary or permanent, and partial or total. On at least three occasions between 1985 and 1992, IBM was prepared to bring out a new product in both the workstation and PC market when its chief competitors Sun and Compaq brought out new, clearly superior products just weeks ahead of IBM. On each occasion, IBM chose to cannibalize its own product rather than weaken its reputation. IBM thus took the loss in R&D and manufacturing investment rather than place a significantly inferior product on the market. In each case, their withdrawal was a temporary maneuver that enabled them to develop a better product (Bryan 1990).

Once a firm has developed an outline of all its competitors' value chains and analyzed its strategic position relative to each competitor, then the firm is in a position to determine the best way to theoretically and practically convert its value chain potential into a strategic capability, which, when linked with customers, will create a sustainable competitive advantage.

A Theory For Converting Value Chain Potential Into Strategic Organizational Capabilities to Yield a Sustainable Competitive Advantage

According to Coyne (1986:26), sustainable competitive advantage exists when "customers perceive a consistent differentiation on important attributes between a producer's product or service and those of his competitors *and that difference is the direct consequence of a capability gap between the producer and his competitors and both the difference in important attributes and the capability gap can be expected to endure over time.*" A capability, according to Stalk et al. (1992:62), "is a set of business processes strategically understood. Every company has business processes that deliver value to the customer. But few think of them as the primary object of strategy."

Capability-based competitors review their value chain in comparison to other competitors and locate those functional and business processes in which they themselves have competitive advantage. They then try to link or coalign those functions and processes in some systematic way, so as to set an industry benchmark that will yield a sustainable competitive advantage. We believe there are three separate and yet combinable theoretic approaches to converting value-added organizational functions and business processes into strategic capabilities, which can establish a world-class benchmark and generate a sustainable competitive advantage: (1) knowledge based coalignment, (2) alliance based coalignment, and (3) technology based coalignment of value-added functions and business processes.

Knowledge-Based Capabilities.   Comparing a firm's value chain with the value chain of all of the firm's competitors involves locating one or more of a value-added organization's functions and/or business processes in which one excels in comparison to one competitors. The question then arises as to how the firm should strategically link and configure those value-added activities with its customers to obtain a sustainable competitive advantage. In such cases, one's own firm's unique knowledge of value-added activities, grouped into capabilities in linking with the customers, yields the sustainable competitive advantage. Then, through a judicious use of a firm's continuous improvement program, these capabilities are focused, linked, and improved to create a sustainable competitive advantage and a new world-class benchmark.

The Toyota Production System (TPS), sometimes called lean production management, illustrates the development of such an internal, knowledge-based capability. Kiichiro Toyoda and Taiichi Ohno led the development of this knowledge based capability. In the 1960s, Toyota appraised the skills of its automotive craftsmen and the standardization and mass production techniques used by Ford Motor Corporation, and then asked their workers to form into small, self-managed, cross-functional teams and integrate these two processes. The goal was to combine the quality of a craftsman with the standardization characterizing mass production. Kiichiro Toyota felt also that each worker on this new line should be trained in several areas, including production tasks, maintenance, recordkeeping, and quality control (Taylor 1990).

Management delegated to workers both the right and the responsibility to continuously improve the process. Next, Toyota formed small cross-functional teams between factory workers and suppliers in order to improve the quality and inventory levels of parts. In what must be considered a breakthrough in creative thinking, these continuous improvement teams came with the Kanban system. Parts were to be inspected at the manufacturer's plants and then shipped to Toyota just in time for use. This in turn substantially reduced the capital tied up in inventory, while reduced costs, increased the turn over ratio on capital, and improved product quality (Womsek, Jones, and Ross 1990).

In the 1980s, Toyota attempted to develop a continuous-flow manufacturing system for turning out small numbers of different low-priced cars. The central problem in achieving this goal was the tooling cost and time needed for custom designed dies to stamp out parts for a car. The tools and machines required for this stamping process form up to 73% of the total cost of a new car. Stamping also accounts for two-thirds of the time needed to build a car. Cross-functional and self-managed teams were set up, and, by employing an international bench-marking against the U.S. auto industry, managed in just three years to cut the cost and time of designing and manufacturing with these dies by one-half to two-thirds when compared to U.S. automakers.

Production processes were simplified and redesigned and the quality improved. Next, Toyota saw the need to reorganize its management system and become more responsive by cutting out two layers of middle management, about 1000 executives. Finally, Toyota divided its product development teams into three groups: (1) small front-wheel drive cars, (2) big rear-wheel drive cars, and (3) trucks. In a creative program aimed at correctly targeting its specific auto models within the three divisions of narrow customer niches, each model was given a chief engineer, who headed a cross-functional team made up or representatives from each functional unit and from business processes in the value chain. This group scanned the customers, competitors, and general economic trends in order to appropriately design, manufacture, and market a new car for its customer niche (Cusumano 1988).

After forty years of focused continuous improvement programs, which employ self-managed and cross-functional teams, benchmarking, and breakthroughs, Toyota's Lean Manufacturing System has become a model for sequencing the value-added aspects of a firm's value chain to form a knowledge-based strategic capability which has created a sustainable competitive advantage. Today, on average, Toyota builds cars and trucks faster, with higher quality, more unique features, and at a lower cost than any of its competitors. Customers have responded to this knowledge-based capability by increasing Toyota's market shares, ranking these cars top in quality and demanding that other producers provide similar standard features (Womack Jones, and Ross 1990).

Whereas knowledge-based capabilities reside totally in the linkages within a firm, as does effective use of continuous improvement programs, alliance-based capabilities reside in the negotiated linkages between firms, and thus lead to effective use of continuous improvement programs.

Alliance-Based Capabilities.   Comparing a firm's value chain with the firm's competitors often reveals that while aspects of a firm's value chain can produce value-added activities, some portions of the firm's value chain, those of most concern to the customer, are not present or do not function at an appropriate level. Under such conditions, an organization may choose to form one or more linking arrangements with other firms who are performing well in these customer sensitive areas, in order to obtain sustainable competitive advantage.

The knowledge necessary to do this resides in an alliance-based strategic capability. Such linkages may take the forms of mergers, acquisitions, equity partnerships, consortia, joint ventures, development agreements, supply agreements, and/or marketing agreements (Nohria and Garcia-Pont 1991: 105). In all cases, however, continuous improvement programs are needed to set up inside, outside, and inter-linkages and to upgrade their performance to create a world-class benchmark.

Successful strategic alliances are few and far between, mainly due to the difficult problems that arise when an important part of a firm's value chain resides either partially or completely within another organization. The Ford Motor Corporation's thirteen-year joint venture with the Mazda Corporation, however, did establish world class benchmarks for both organizations in two different areas, and as such warrants our close attention.

In 1979, Ford and Mazda Corporations formed a joint venture to cooperate on the development of new vehicles and to share valuable expertise. Ford was to share product design, international marketing, and finance expertise with Mazda, and Mazda was to share product development and manufacturing expertise with Ford. Both firms were to remain totally autonomous in this joint venture. They were to undertake only those cooperative projects that had mutual benefits. This was to be judged on a project-by-project basis. Early on the need for a set of operating rules, a set of coordination rules and an impartial outside arbitrator for disputes became evident. Mazda President Wadra and Ford President Bouton outlined these operating rules (Treece, Miller, and Melcher 1992:104):

1. Keep management involved. The boss must set a tone for the relationship. Otherwise middle managers will resist ceding partial control of a project to a partner.

2. Meet often informally. Meetings should be at all levels and should include time for socializing. Trust can't be built solely around a boardroom table.

3. Use a matchmaker. A third party can mediate disputes, suggest new ways of approaching the partner, and offer an independent sounding board.

4. Maintain your independence. Independence helps both parties hone the areas of expertise that made them desirable partners in the first place.

5. Allow no 'sacrifice' deals. Every project must be viable for each partner. It is up to senior management to see than an overall balance is maintained.

6. Appoint a monitor. Someone must take primary responsibility for monitoring all aspects of an alliance.

7. Anticipate cultural differences. They may be corporate, or national. Stay flexible, and try to place culturally sensitive executives in key posts.

A four-man monitoring group then set up and established the following coordination rules: 1.) This group is in daily contact with each other by computer and must meet face at least once every eight months. 2.) Four months after this group's face-to-face meeting, Ford and Mazda's chairmen and staff must meet to review the progress of ongoing projects. 3.) Twice a year the heads of each firm's product development and manufacturing units must meet. 4.) Self-managed, cross-functional, and international benchmarking teams for each project should work together on a daily basis. (Treece, Miller, and Melcher 1992:104).

Finally, a member of the Sumitomo Bank of Japan was selected as the impartial arbitrator for unresolvable disputes. Such disputes arose frequently in the early years of the joint venture and then disappeared entirely (Treece, Miller, and Melcher 1992: 103). Ford and Mazda's joint venture has helped each firm establish world-class organizational capabilities in previously weak areas of their respective value chains. For example, today one in every four cars sold in the United States have benefited from some degree of Mazda's help, while two of every five Mazdas sold have received help from Ford. In addition, Ford obtained access to Mazda's distribution capabilities in Japan, became the largest seller (72,000) of U.S. cars last year in Japan, and modeled its super-efficient Hermosilla, Mexico plant on the design of a Mazda plant located in Japan (Treece, Miller, and Melcher 1992:103). Today, Ford's Mexico manufacturing plant, thanks to Mazda, is outpacing all other U. S. and Japanese corporations in reducing product cost and increasing product quality (Lohr 1992, D2). Today, Mazda's auto designs, marketing and finance with the help of Ford has led to a dramatic increase in Mazda's auto shares (Treece, Miller, and Melcher 1992: 104).

Technology-Based Capabilities.   In comparing a firm's value chain with the firm's competitors, one may find that while some aspects of a firm's value chain can produce value-added activities, some portions of a firm's value chain of most concern to the customers cannot do so without the addition of some new state-of-the-art technology. Under such conditions, the firm's entire value chain may be in need of modification in order to reap the benefits of this new technology.

The knowledge necessary to obtain this value-added advantage resides in the innovative and appropriate use of these new technologies. In all cases, continuous improvement programs are necessary to implement the new technologies and to appropriately adjust the value chain to the technology so as not to lose other value-added gains. The list of corporations who have attempted to leapfrog competition but failed to do so include GM, IBM, and AT&T. However, one such attempt which has led to dramatic success is that of The Limited.

The Limited Company is a major manufacturer of women's apparel throughout the world. Each evening, the store managers in 3,200 stores across the United States collect data regarding sales for that day—size, color, fashion number, and so forth—through their Electronic Point Sale computer system (EPOS). The cutting order information is telecommunicated to the Limited's workshops in Hong Kong, Singapore, and Sri Lanka, and is translated into next-day manufacturing orders. Within days, these just-in-time inventory replacements are shipped to the Limited's Ohio distribution center on a Boeing 747 (Macrae 1988: 15).

In addition to supplying replacement merchandise in a timely fashion, the Limited EPOS system can be used to monitor marketing. It can track fashion design performance, pinpointing age groups, income level, and geographic locations where specific fashion designs sell well. Ultimately, EPOS could be used for ordering customized designs by color, size, cut, and style, with less than one week of turnaround on delivery of orders. In the use of EPOS Merchandising for customized design, computer-integrated manufacturing fused into a flexible, high-speed, reciprocally coordinated interface system (Phillips and Denkin 1989: 192). The Limited has diversified its business in 1990 by acquiring Lerner, Victoria's Secret, Lane Bryant, and opening The Limited express. In each of these chains, EPOS has been employed as a value-added tool for successfully dominating their respective market niches (Phillips and Denkin 1989:199).

Finally, "the Limited's mass merchandisers can take the newest trends from Paris or New York and place cheaper versions in its stores weeks before the original designs are produced" (Hochswender 1990: 5). This provides The Limited with a technology based capability for dominating its respective markets.

Combination-based coalignment. Many portions of a firm's value chain must link with other firms in order to obtain some knowledge-based, some alliance-based, and some technology-based capabilities. In such cases, the focal organization may enter into numerous linking arrangements between parts of its organization and parts of others in order to capitalize on the value-added activities of all the firms.

IBM recently experienced its first loss of income in over fifty years. In an effort to respond quickly to these losses and become more profitable, IBM decentralized their management system, cut personnel, and allowed the decentralized organizations to enter into alliances with other firms in an attempt to strengthen their core capabilities.

In an attempt to increase their knowledge-based, alliance-based and technology-based core capabilities, IBM entered into four types of alliances. Knowledge-based, or strategic alliances were formed with Stratus, Motorola, Apple, Novell, Borland, Lotus, AT&T, and Systems Application Architecture. Technology-based alliances were formed with Motorola, Compaq, Apple, Intel, Sybase, Borland, Lotus, and Systems Application Architecture. Alliance-based relationships were formed through equity partnerships and joint ventures with IBM equity partners and Apple. Finally, IBM broke off its joint venture with Microsoft over the Microsoft Windows program, which competed directly with IBM's OS/2. IBM is currently involved in over 1000 negotiated linking arrangements with other firms aimed at enhancing all its core capabilities.

Capability-based competitors review their value chain in comparison to their competitors, locate those functional and business processes in which they have competitive advantage and then try to link or coalign those functions or processes in some systematic way so as to set world-class benchmarks that will yield sustainable competitive advantage through (1) knowledge based, (2) alliance based, (3) technology based, and (4) combination based coalignment. Continuous improvement programs are then employed to generate and maintain sustainable competitive advantage. Toyota, Ford, and The Limited each employed capabilities analysis, as outlined above, to obtain a recognizable, sustainable competitive advantage from its knowledge-based, alliance-based and technology-based capabilities.

A NEGOTIATED LINKING PROGRAM'S CRITICAL SUCCESS FACTORS

A strategic vision pulls together the insights obtained from examining the multiple scenarios, the industry's competitive structure, and the firm's (and competitor's) distinct core capabilities. It helps to focus managerial attention and indicate which core capabilities the firm must develop further and how, so as to succeed in its chosen business segments. (Schoemaker 1992:76)

Senior executives frequently ponder such questions as "what might give us a sustainable competitive advantage?" The answer provided here is that firms must use world-class core capabilities in areas of customer need. We have presented the following four-step analysis of the critical success factors involved in establishing such a core capability:

1. an environmental scanning analysis of:

   a. What are your business global market dynamics today and in the near future?

   b. What actions have your competitors taken in the last three years to influence those global dynamics?

   c. What have you done in the last three years to influence those dynamics?

   d. What are the most dangerous things your competitors could do in the next three years to influence those dynamics?

   e. What are the most effective things you can do to bring about the desired impact on those dynamics?

2. What strategy should our firm employ in dealing with each of our competitors?

   a. confront

   b. focus

   c. circumvent

   d. join

   e. withdraw

3. How can our value chain capabilities be converted into strategic organizational capabilities when linked with customers to create a sustainable competitive advantage?

4. A firm's goal is to develop those core capabilities through continuous improvement programs that will be effective in multiple market segments of the industry's alternative potential futures. The effective coalignment of those core capabilities is thus the key to success. Continuous improvement programs are the key to effective coalignment.

We began this chapter by noting that a firm's strategic fit with its environment was the key to corporate success in the 1990's. We noted that tight fit led to sustained excellent performance. We now see that knowledge-based, alliance-based, technology-based, and combination-based capabilities generate a tight fit, creating the underlying dynamic necessary for producing excellence in negotiated linking processes.

SEVEN

Breakthroughs: Future Mapping

> When the competitive advantage
> gained from new management prac-
> tices lessens, because of their in-
> creasingly universal application, a few
> firms seeking new competitive advan-
> tage, begin charting the course to yet
> another business-wide transition or
> management era. Eventually, succes-
> sive business-wide transition and
> management eras begin producing
> only marginal advantages and bene-
> fits, thus setting the stage for a
> fundamental shift or transformation.
> Hickman and Silva (1987: 8)

We stressed in Chapter 2 that adaptation is a hallmark of
successful companies. Until now we concentrated on the first
test of adaptation: aligning the organization to the challenges,
opportunities, and threats of its environment via external linkages, benchmarking, and cross-functional and self-managed
teamwork. Skillful management of the continuous improvement
process leads to the coalignment of the organization and its
environment through constant and usually incremental refine-
ments. This ongoing approach is the essence of the Japanese
version of continuous improvement: the *kaizen* movement. The
Japanese style of continuous improvement consists of literally
millions of small, constant, and mundane improvements developed and implemented by all organizational members every year
(Imai 1986).

Such an approach is particularly suitable to relatively stable environments. However, research on both organizational successes (Peters and Waterman 1982) and failures (Meyer and Zucker 1989) has shown that in the type of turbulent environments that most business organizations face today, dramatic and rapid breakthroughs are necessary. A less gradual approach is necessary to shake up the organization; change its adaptation pattern; promote coalignment with new environmental forces, trends and patterns; and create a new framework for continuous incremental improvements. Thus, long periods of improvement and alignments should be punctuated with discontinuous reorientation in order to maintain an overall momentum of change (Tushman, Newman, and Romanelli 1986). In this chapter we will illustrate the importance and strategies of such frame-breaking change.

More specifically, we shall (1) define the concept of breakthrough and explain the major stimulating forces; and (2) explore the main strategies of breakthrough in terms of scope, thrust, and character. Finally, we will illustrate how different breakthrough strategies sustain and/or change an organization's competitive advantage, creating a new frame for subsequent incremental improvements.

THE CONCEPT OF BREAKTHROUGHS

While large amounts of research in many different countries, industries, and company sizes deal with the concept of breakthrough, its precise definition is difficult to determine. We use here the definition given by Tushman, Newman, and Romannelli (1986: 31): *a simultaneous and sharp shift in strategy, power, structure, and controls.*

There are abundant company histories, case studies, and research that illustrate the evolutionary patterns of organizational life cycles. One of the first such studies was Chandler's (1962) seminal study of strategy and structure elations in large American firms such as DuPont, General Motors and Sears. After tracking the evolution of several firms, Chandler persuasively concluded that successful companies, at an important moment in their history (for example, in a time of crisis), are able to develop a significant strategic breakthrough, which in turn enables them to catch up and keep pace with or dominate their respective industries for years. Two classic examples are General Motors' marketing strategy and DuPont's divisional structure. GM experienced a breakthrough when it created five generic segments of the car market supplied by its Chevrolet, Pontiac, Oldsmobile, Buick, and Cadillac divisions. DuPont succeeded with its new and powerful organizational model, which consisted of a distribution of responsibility and competence along divisional lines.

The importance of creative breakthroughs was confirmed in several other research studies. Miller and Friesen (1984) reported on a series of studies that covered "quantum changes" in more than forty firms from diverse industries. A joint research program coming from Columbia, Duke, and Cornell Universities tracked the history of a large sample of firms in different industries, finding that most successful firms experience a similar evolutionary pattern: long periods of incremental improvements are punctuated by major changes (Tushman, Newman, and Romanelli 1986). An analysis performed by Slatter (1986) in the United Kingdom of a large sample of case studies found that corporate recovery is a mix of incremental changes and marketing, financial, and organizational breakthroughs.

A unique situation that enabled the monitoring of adaptive firm behavior occurred, in the early 1990s, in the post-communist countries of Eastern and Central Europe, where the business environment underwent a dramatic change from a planned to a free-market economy. State-owned firms scrambled to adapt to this new situation. Research shows that most of the state-owned firms in Poland and Hungary have been unable to adapt to the changes in economic structure. They have been developing incrementally rather than effecting the breakthrough changes necessary to respond to a dramatic shift in the environment (Obloj and Davis 1991; Connor and Ploszajski 1992; Kozminski 1993). What differentiates incremental change from breakthroughs? The two primary defining characteristics are speed and multi-dimensionality.

Main Features of Breakthroughs

Rapid. Breakthroughs occur swiftly, in response to the environmental turbulence created by competitors' actions and customers' changing demands. As already discussed, from the customer's perspective today's markets share characteristics of quick saturation, a shrinking product-life cycle, the convergence of consumer tastes and needs, and volatility in market segments and niches. The competitive environment is characterized by increasing hostility, complexity, and rate of change. All of these elements make for environmental turbulence, which requires a rapid response.

Multi-Dimensional. Breakthroughs require some degree of conformity throughout the organization, as they require *simultaneous* change in several important areas of the organization's performance. Even if one dimension (for example, marketing or technology) is a major source and focus of breakthrough, as the adaptive effort is directed toward particular environmental demands, it must be co-aligned with other organizational changes creating a new pattern of action.

Having established these two features as common to all organizational breakthroughs, we shall now turn to a discussion of the four main breakthrough strategies.

STRATEGIES OF BREAKTHROUGH

Developing a breakthrough strategy requires that two standard choices be made, both of which are related to thrust and scope. A firm can: (1) reorient its thrust toward either beating its competitor or better satisfying the needs of its customers, and (2) choose either a focused or diffused scope of strategic breakthrough. Let us review these choices and then illustrate how they are combined by firms in order to create winning breakthrough strategies.

Orientation

The first strategic choice was stressed by K. Ohmae (1982; 1988). He argues that companies may choose between two main thrusts in developing their strategies. They can orient their action *against* the competitor in a head-on or more subtle attack, or *toward* customers in the search for better ways to satisfy their needs. Even if sometimes there is considerable overlap between these thrusts, the difference between them is still fundamental. In the first approach, competitors serve as the benchmarks, while in the second approach, customers perform this role.

Competitor-Driven. A firm that uses the competitor-driven approach assesses competitive goods or services and strives to offer better and differentiated products. The ongoing competitive battle among American, German, and Japanese car makers illustrates such competitive benchmarking. Japanese car makers first chose as their strategic target the mass market segment dominated by American companies; they succeeded in this market by offering more durable cars at a lower price. In the late 1980s, Japanese car makers moved upscale and directly attacked the position of German car makers such as Mercedes and BMW by producing the Lexus and Infinity models. In this second case, both the type of cars and marketing efforts served as competitive breakthroughs in the upper-scale market. While customers are still important in a competitor-driven strategic thrust, the company's competitors are the strategic frame of reference when planning the market launch.

Consumer-Driven. Firms launch consumer-driven breakthroughs by paying painstaking attention to the needs of customers in order to better serve them. As a result, companies are able to develop superior or completely innovative products and services, as in the case of the unique Matsushita bread-making machine (see Nonaka, 1991) or the Chrysler mini-van. Customers come first; competitive realities are relegated to a secondary position.

Scope

Focused. The second strategic choice related to the scope of the breakthrough in terms of its being focused or diffused. A focused breakthrough can be defined as a well-developed resource or capability that serves as the basis for a competitive advantage. Even as a focused breakthrough creates resounding effects throughout the organization, it can be easily identified and analyzed. Polaroid's proprietary technology, Honda's competencies in engine development and production, and Coca-Cola's brand name are typical examples of such a particular resource or capability.

Diffused. Diffused breakthroughs are different. They create a system of durable capabilities diffused throughout the organization; they are, therefore, difficult for competitors to understand, identity, and imitate. The logistical system developed by Wal-Mart, the lean manufacturing system of Toyota, or the active, value-based management system of Body Shop International are clear illustrations of such breakthroughs. All three breakthroughs were achieved by creating resources and capabilities that were diffused throughout the whole organization via being embedded in technical and social aspects of performance. These capabilities can be difficult to identify, but each of the firms has clear ownership and control over them.

The two strategic choices related to the way that companies leapfrog the competition and punctuate their improvement drive are illustrated in Table 7.1. Let us now illustrate the successful application of each of these strategies with case studies.

STRATEGY IN PRACTICE

Competitor-Oriented, Focused Breakthrough

The logic of the competitor-oriented and focused breakthrough is similar to that of a classic offensive strategic move. The organization analyzes and benchmarks its competitor's product or service with a limited market scope. The new, dramatically improved product concept developed from this analysis is broken down into hundreds of tasks that must be executed in a timely fashion. The teams' structure is usually built around tasks, with project coordinators monitoring the progress of the project as a whole. If successful, such an approach usually changes the market rules of the game and puts the firm that pioneered the offensive move ahead of its competitors.

Table 7.1. Generic Breakthrough Strategies

	STRATEGIC TARGET	
	Competitor	Consumer
Focused scope	Competitor-oriented, focused breakthrough	Consumer-oriented, focused breakthrough
Diffused scope	Competitor-oriented, diffused breakthrough	Consumer-oriented, diffused breakthrough

Most high-image companies serving the top segments of the market make the same classic marketing mistake at least once. They introduce an affordable, low-end model lacking most of the features of their more advanced and expensive models. The rationale of such an entry is simple. The high-end supplier hopes to broaden the scope of the market, and thereby increase profits and improve cash flow. Almost invariably the results are contrary to expectations: the product is a dud and the image of the producer is at least temporarily tarnished, as in the cases of Nikon's cheap camera, Porsche's low-end model, and Helena Rubinstein's affordable perfumes. Even if the product is relatively successful, as in the case of Mercedes 190 (nicknamed the Mercedes-Baby), the entry into low-end market segments is dangerous. It dilutes the company's image and makes the original market niche vulnerable to potential attack by competitors.

Such was the case with the United States' introduction of low-end cars from European luxury producers, especially Mercedes, at the beginning of the 1980s. The Japanese car makers entered the luxury car segments and developed upscale cars to compete in the market segments that were previously inaccessible, primarily due to the luxury producer's consistent brand image.

Case: Lexus.   The preparation, and introduction to the market of Toyota's Lexus car will surely become a classic case of the competitor-oriented, focused breakthrough. Lexus was a car directly targeted at the limited (about one million units) U.S. luxury car market. In addition to being limited in scope, the breakthrough can be classified as a competitor-oriented one for three reasons: (1) it was directly targeted against two European car makers that symbolize the high-end market segment, namely, Mercedes-Benz and BMW, whose best cars served as benchmarks for the team developing the Lexus; (2) initial sales of Lexus directly affected Mercedes and BMW as they lost market share; and (3) Lexus (and Nissan's Infinity) redefined the market in the luxury market by offering better value for the money, which put European car-makers on the defensive.

Toyota is currently the third largest car-maker in the world after General Motors and Ford (Taylor 1991). It holds over 45 percent of the market in Japan, and almost 7 percent in the U.S..[10] Toyota enjoys the highest operating margin in the global auto industry, and is considered a role model for a well-managed company. The company's great strength lies in the fact that though it rarely is the first with a new product type, it almost always succeeds in catching up by developing a product better than that of its competitors.

Development of the Lexus started in 1983, when Toyota executives recognized the opportunity to enter the luxury car segment which in the United States has traditionally been dominated by European producers. Lacking the proper image of a luxury car producer, Toyota relied on marketing overkill by designing a car substantially cheaper and better than its benchmarked rivals. Taylor (1989: 62–63) explains Toyota's strategy: "Toyota set out to do what nobody else had done: design a sedan that would travel 150 mph while carrying four passengers in relative quiet, comfort and safety—and without incurring the American gas-guzzler tax...Those specifications dictated breakthroughs in aerodynamics, noise dampening, suspension, and most of all, the engine."

Development of the Lexus took six years. The development process can be divided into two overlapping stages: (1) technical development and (2) marketing system development.

Technical Development Stage.   The extremely high performance parameters of the Lexus stretched the limits of Toyota's engineering and manufacturing capabilities (Taylor 1989; Taylor 1990). To ensure tight coupling of engineering and manufacturing, each major component was developed by special Flagship Quality Committees. At the beginning of each individual project the designers led the committees. As the project neared production, manufacturing specialists became the committee leaders. Toyota designed a completely new 32–valve, aluminum block V–8 engine with extreme operating efficiency characteristics. The first prototypes met the technical requirements but consumed too much gasoline. In order to limit the gasoline intake, the engine was dismantled and most of the components redesigned and improved with engine efficiency in mind. The shape and weight of every car component (even the tires!) were taken into account in order to increase the efficiency. However, the focus remained on reducing the air-drag influence without comprising the limousine- and Mercedes-like look. Constant experimentation resulted in a 0.29 drag coefficient, which is one of the best of any car on the market. Prototype versions of the Lexus were tested for over three years throughout the world in different climates, on different roads, until they totaled almost two million miles (the industry standard is about one million miles). The final effect of the detailed, well integrated development stage was a car of exceptional quality and high performance with superior acceleration and mileage parameters.

Marketing Stage.   Marketing research and analysis were simultaneous with technical development. In 1985, Toyota designers traveled throughout the United States using marketing research techniques to discover customers needs and wants. They were trying to discover how to persuade German car buyers to purchase a Japanese luxury car. Every detail and piece of information was analyzed; every feature of design (including seat leather and console wood samples) was selected with the utmost care.

Three crucial marketing decisions proved to have the greatest influence on the car's success. First, Toyota executives decided to built a special dealer network, equipped with new showrooms and repair shops, to distinguish Lexus from other Toyota brands and thereby enhance its "special car" image. The decision proved correct, as it helped to build a separate Lexus brand image. Second, Lexus changed the definition of a "standard" version of a car. Almost every car around the world is sold in a standard version, with options sold separately. In the case of luxury cars, especially Mercedes, BMW, and Porsche, these options are both expensive and numerous, and range from an improved sound system to leather-covered keys. Toyota executives decided to break this pattern and include most of the options as part of Lexus' standard version (for example, an upgraded sound system tuned separately for different types of upholstery, a remote start system). Third, the company, contrary to its usual practices, decided to run a long press preview with great fanfare it its main competitor's backyard: Germany. Journalists were offered Jaguars, Mercedes, and BMWs to drive and compare. Lexus came out of the tests a winner.

The combined efforts of detailed technical development and skillful marketing resulted in a car that proved a superb competitive weapon. Launched in the United States in September 1989, Lexus sold almost 20,000 cars the same year, far exceeding the target of 8,000 cars. Meanwhile, sales of Mercedes and BMW decreased in the United States. From a high in 1988, when Mercedes sold about 83,000 cars and BMW almost 74,000, sales dropped in 1991 to 55,000 for Mercedes and 50,000 for BMW. During the same period the sales of Lexus increased to 70,000 in 1991 and 80,000 the following year. Thus, during 1991, only two years after its introduction, Lexus sales were 21% higher than those of Mercedes and 29 percent higher those of BMW.

The image of Lexus as the perfect luxury car was enhanced by the quality problems it encountered after the 1989 launch. Two complaints were filed during the first two months: one owner's cruise control would not turn off and another's center brake light melted. Toyota converted these quality problems into an opportunity to demonstrate the convenience and commitment of its postsale service. Each owner was offered a choice: bring in the car yourself to be fixed on the spot, or have Lexus pick it up at night and return it the next morning. Cars were returned fixed, inspected, cleaned, and filled with gas. The whole operation enhanced the Lexus image among customers and put pressure on other luxury car producers to match Lexus's service.

Let us reiterate the lessons we can gather from the Lexus example of a focused, competitor-oriented breakthrough strategy. First, Toyota used its competitors' introduction of low-end cars as an opportunity to enter the limited luxury car segment. Second, it used the best cars of its competitors as benchmarks, designing and producing cars that were superior in terms of quality, technical parameters, standard equipment, and price. Third, in order to achieve a new fit of culture, strategy, and processes, it established a separate brand, dealers, and service network for the product. However, the fact that Lexus is produced by Toyota is well-known. The association was mutually beneficial: it lent credibility to the Lexus design, quality, and service from the beginning, while later Lexus's new role as market leader enhanced Toyota's image.

Consumer-Oriented, Focused Breakthrough

The core of consumer-oriented and focused breakthroughs is a standard marketing practice: a market niche, or product/service or even a marketing tool are examined and consumers behavior and needs analyzed from different perspectives in search of a new an innovative approach. An example of such a breakthrough development is the simple idea of *control over discount coupons* introduced by Catalina system.

Case: Catalina Marketing.   Discount coupons are an old marketing technique very popular in the United States and rapidly catching on in Europe. The essence of discount coupons is simple: by offering a special bargain, producers hope to lure customers who will later repeat the purchase. The greatest weakness of this marketing technique lies in its lack of focus on the target market due to imperfections in distribution. Typical distribution of coupons via mail or newspapers is always imprecise, if not almost random. Coupons often fail to reach potential customers, others are offered to people with no interest in the product, while still other coupons are given to customers who already buy the brand. Many coupons fail to build brand loyalty, and instead only marginally and temporally influence shopping patterns.

These disadvantages of coupons have been well known, but only recently Catalina Marketing, a California-based company, developed a breakthrough system that allows companies to focus coupons on particular type of customer. In this way they are able to diminish, at least partially, the major problems that occur with using coupons as a marketing tool. Catalina Marketing offers a computer system that monitors the flow of data from the cash-register scanners at supermarkets and prints out a coupon when triggered. The system can be programmed in various ways. The most typical application is to print a coupon for a product currently being purchased in order to reinforce brand loyalty. Coupons can also be offered for complementary products (for example, a toothpaste purchase will trigger the printing of coupons for a toothbrush) or to boost the store's sales and image (a certain level of store purchases causes coupons to be printed for free food at the store deli). Finally, coupon disbursement can be also used as a competitive weapon. Coupons for a particular product can be printed and offered to the purchaser of a competing brand in order to encourage brand switching (as when Colgate toothpaste buyers receive a Crest coupon).

The innovative nature of this marketing system lies in the simultaneous integration of three features: flexibility, measurability, and precision. It is a flexible system because it can be programmed to allow different coupons to be printed for different customers under different contingencies. The system also is measurable, because it enables the user to control most of the important marketing variables. Finally, Catalina's system is precise because it allows the user to focus his marketing strategy on a particular type of customer or purchasing behavior. (The Economist, September 5, 1992: 66).

Consumer-Oriented, Diffused Breakthroughs

Diffused breakthroughs, both consumer- and customer-oriented, are more difficult to analyze for research purposes and more difficult competitors to imitate. The essence of such break-throughs is the development of set of unique, difficult to imitate resources or capabilities spread throughout the organization and reaching out into its environment. The consumer orientation of such breakthroughs causes the firm to differentiate in many ways that are visible and valued by both customers and other businesses, as in the case of Body Shop International. In a 1992 study performed by the *Economist* and Laughborough University Business School, the company received a rank of 13 in a general ranking of Britain's most admired companies.

Case: Body Shop International. When Anita Roddick founded The Body Shop International in the United Kingdom, she unknowingly followed the favorite axiom of Sam Walton, America's greatest merchant: break all the rules. She expressed this rule in a different way by stating that to be a success in business one must be daring, be first, be different. And while most managers think that profit is exciting, business is important, and social concerns are tiresome, Anita Roddick thinks otherwise. From her perspective, social issues are important, business is exciting, and profits are indispensable but boring.

In 1976 she decided to go into the difficult and competitive business of cosmetics, once described cynically as the business of producing goods and selling hope. She started with a $6,400 bank loan for a small shop that became an extremely successful company: The Body Shop International. The story of Anita Roddick's entrepreneurial success is unique, however, because the marketing and management foundations of The Body Shop International are different from those of a traditional company in three respects: (1) the company is run both as a business operation and an idealistic social movement, trying to spark the interest of both employees and customers; (2) the marketing principles differentiate the company from its competitors by providing customers with information instead of promotion and ads; and (3) the management process is oriented toward preservation of the start-up spirit.

Merging ideals and business. The Body Shop is an unusual mix of business operation and social movement. The firm starts and supports a series of ecological and social campaigns, including efforts to save the whales, to save the Amazon rain- forest or the Yanomani Indians (a Stone Age tribe dying out in Brazil), and to oppose the repression of political dissidents. The business activities, combined with the political, social, and ecological issues build a densely interwoven framework of The Body Shop and its employees' engagement and committment. The combination also stimulates general public interest and support. Other companies try to incorporate activism; many of them support worldwide organizations fighting for a good cause. The uniqueness of The Body Shop's approach lies in the fact that it incorporates the idealism of values and the fight for a better, cleaner, more peaceful world into the business in order to create strong bonds, passion, and an almost missionary zeal among its employees and customers. Anita Roddick describes her methods (Burlingham 1990: 42):

I'd never get that kind of motivation if we were just selling shampoo and body lotion. I'd never get that sort of staying late, talking at McDonald's after work, bonding to customers. It's a way for people to bond to the company. They're doing what I'm doing. They're learning. Three years ago I didn't know anything about the rain forest. Five years ago I didn't know anything about the ozone layer. It's a process of learning to be a global citizen. And what it produces is a sense of passion you simply won't find in a Bloomingdale's department store.

Thus, the skillful and passionate combination of values and business has three important results: (1) it motivates, rejuve- nates and inspires employees; (2) it creates important bonds with value-oriented customers; and (3) it signifies the strong belief of the company founders and managers that companies should identify and help to solve important social problems by getting directly involved. It should not be surprising that The Body Shop is consistently recognized in Britain's community and environmental responsibility rankings.

Marketing. The Body Shop's marketing strategy runs counter to the industry patterns that rely on brand image, fancy packaging, heavy promotions, and skillful advertisement. The company does not advertise its products heavily, direct promo- tion is limited, and packaging is, for the most part, plain. The company relies primarily on the force of pure information about the product (for example, ingredients, how they are combined and in what process, how, they are tested, and so forth) that is shared with customers. However, the information is supported by the actual use of special ingredients and production techniques, as well as by special employee training to establish credibility and product benefits.

All ingredients used for production purposes are natural and have been used by humans in different countries for many years, which practically eliminates the need to test the final product. The firm makes a point of notifying its customers with a message on all product containers: Not Tested on Animals.

The Body Shop empowers and trains its employees by creating a superb educational system. The firm's training center in London focuses almost exclusively on teaching all employees and franchisees the nature and uses of the product, and on building their knowledge base and molding attitudes. The information/facts-center training is continually reinforced with videos, brochures, posters, and newsletters reminding employees that they are in a knowledge-based business, that customers matter, and that there are more important things than profitability.

Preserving entrepreneurial spirit. Anita Roddick knows that as companies grow from the start-up stage into a more mature business, they follow a typical life cycle. As the new venture matures and grows, new employees are hired and their responsibility and tasks are defined. Structure is developed with levels of management and functional departments. Control and reporting systems, like management information systems, are put in place. Long-term business plans are developed. Investments are made. During this process, most entrepreneurs and organizations loose their naivete and dreams and become orderly, moneymaking machines.

The Body Shop International tries to break away from this normal pattern in several ways. First, as we have already described, the company tries to preserve the original values and ideals on which it was started by adhering to its base of natural products and shops as places promoting natural skin and hair care. The firm is committed to preserving this image. Any effort to dilute or sacrifice it for growth or profit requirements is unacceptable. Second, by starting and/or supporting campaigns on important environmental and social issues, the company keeps passions and emotions at a high level. The company uses all possible means such as posters, window displays, T-shirts, training, brochures, videotapes, slide shows, and even Body Shop employee demonstrations to focus on various social issues such as support for the inhabitants of the Amazon rain forests. Third, the entrepreneurial spirit is maintained through Anita Roddick's leadership style: energetic, passionate, and direct. She creates a role model of excitement and commitment that people want to follow. These three factors work to create a visibly entrepreneurial company. In the 1992 study of Britain's most admired companies, the Body Shop was ranked second only to Glaxo International in terms of the company's innovative capacity.

Let us reiterate the major factors of the diffused, consumer-oriented breakthrough apparent in The Body Shop case. The most obvious aspect is that it is difficult to pinpoint the exact reasons for The Body Shop's commercial and social success. Each of the elements mentioned in the case form part of a complex puzzle that must be pieced together to explain The Body Shop's success. As a firm, it offered a different concept of cosmetics and the way they are sold. In a sense, the firm returned to the basics of business and served the fundamental needs of hair and skin protection and care. Natural ingredients, simple packaging, and full information replaced the mystery, fancy boxes, and heavy promotions typical in the industry. The Body Shop merged business, politics, and social drama in an unusual way to create a dynamic, highly visible sociotechnical system. The firm set up a complicated educational system to train and educate employees and, indirectly, customers, about natural cosmetics and ecology, politics, and social issues. Finally, the firm has a unique leader who manages business and values at high speed. So while it may be relatively easy to imitate each of these elements separately, the magic of The Body Shop breakthrough lies in the fact that the company created a blend that is difficult to replicate.

Competitor-Oriented, Diffused Breakthrough

The essence of a diffused, competitor-oriented break-through is the development of a set of unique and difficult to imitate resources and capabilities spread through the organization. These resources and capabilities enable the company to compete successfully against much more powerful competitors. In short, this type of breakthrough is illustrated by the unprecedented success of the Wal-Mart stores.

Even though discount stores operated for years in the United States, it was only in 1962 that the discount store industry was truly born. Four chains were started that year: the S. S. Kresge chain started Kmart stores; Woolworth started the Woolco chain; Dayton-Hudson opened the first Target store, and the independent operator, Sam Walton, opened his Wal-Mart in Rogers, Arkansas. In 1992, Wal-Mart was the largest retailer in the world, with annual sales exceeding $55 billion and growing, operating 1750 stores and opening around 100 new stores annually. The market value of the company exceeded $50 billion. An explanation of such a phenomenal growth rate, in a business where margins are slim and competition keen, is not simple. However, two success factors stand out. First, as is the case with every good corporation, Wal-Mart was always sensitive to its customers needs for low prices and good quality. Its strategy of "everyday low prices", big stores in convenient locations, and a motivated and inspired workforce are definitely important parts of the success story. However, here we will concentrate on the second, almost invisible factor that the Boston Consulting Group leaders considered a perfect competitive weapon: Wal-Mart's superb, complex logistic system (Stalk, Evans, and Shulman 1992).

Case: Wal-Mart.   Sam Walton, the founder of Wal-Mart, was fond of breaking all textbook rules and following different paths that did his competitors. Stalk et al. (1992: 59) described this aspect of the Wal-Mart struggle with its major competitor, Kmart:

> While Wal-Mart was building its ground transportation fleet, Kmart was moving out of trucking because a subcontracted fleet was cheaper. While Wal-Mart was building close relationships with its suppliers, Kmart was constantly switching suppliers in search of price improvements. While Wal-Mart was controlling all the departments in its stores, Kmart was leasing out many of its departments to other companies on the theory that it could make more per square foot in rent than through its own efforts.

Nevertheless, while breaking most of the rules, there is one that Sam Walton never broke: treat a business as a complex, dynamic system. The consequence of his systemic perspective was *a drive to lower the costs across the system rather than within its parts.* Wal-Mart's major breakthrough is its system of keeping its costs low as compared to its competitors. The system has several important components: low overheads, regional distribution centers, a computerized information system, decentralized decision making, the Wal-Mart truck fleet, and cross-docking.

Low overheads. Wal-Mart has had the lowest ratio of expenses to sales in the retail industry for the last 25 years because Sam Walton considered every dollar valuable and important: "Every time Wal-mart spends one dollar foolishly, it comes right out of our customer's pockets. Every time we save them a dollar, that puts us one more step ahead of the competition - where we always plan to be" (Fortune 1992: 100).

This policy has many practical implications. Wal-Mart's headquarters is one of the most spartan in the country, expenses on promotion are kept low, management perks are scarce, company employees stay in cheap motels and inns, eat at family restaurants, and strive to save money for their customers. The company tries to minimize the number of employees who do not have direct contact with customers.

Regional distribution centers. Wal-Mart created a network of nineteen huge computerized distribution centers. The centers are an intermediary between a set of Wal-Mart suppliers and 1650 stores. The distribution centers are located in such a way that all stores are within a one-day truck drive from one of the regional distribution centers. They are almost fully computerized—the incoming orders trigger the labeling of the packages that are later directed, via laser scanner control, through the warehouse into the right dock and trucks.

Computerized information system. Wal-Mart runs an elaborate, multi-level computerized information system. On the management level, a video link connects all stores to headquarters and to each other. Store managers can hold video conferences and pass detailed and timely information on recent consumer behaviors and trends. On the logistical level, Wal-Mart's operations are monitored by a network of computers. Using a laser pen, a store employee can indicate the type of goods that sell well and should be replenished. This information is checked with information coming from the laser scanners at the cashiers, after which orders are produced and passed to the distribution centers, which in turn pass the orders to more than 4,000 vendors. In this way, point-of-sale data are directly transferred to vendors in a matter of hours, enabling high-speed adaptation of the whole system. The fact that Wal-Mart's vendors are better and faster informed than are competitors' vendors allows them to react more quickly and effectively.

Decentralized decision making. Most retail chains centralize such fundamental decisions as merchandising, pricing and promotions by following a logic of "product push" (Stalk et al. 1992). In comparison, Wal-Mart is decentralized to allow district managers, store managers, and store department heads to have significant decision-making power. Customers regulate the system themselves through increased or decreased levels of purchases, which are registered by computers and employees. Wal-Mart can react instantly to these changes in purchase behavior (for example, price reduction or new orders).

Truck fleet. Wal-Mart operates a huge fleet of trucks that links vendors, distribution centers, and stores on an almost daily basis. On the average, Wal-Mart store shelves are restocked twice a week, while the industry standard is once every two weeks (Stalk et al. 1992: 58). Having its own fleet of trucks gives Wal-Mart greater flexibility and higher-speed reactions than its competitors.

Cross-docking. Cross-docking is a fluid, constant, and efficient flow of goods from vendors' docks to the distribution centers' docks and then to the stores. All of these elements of the Wal-Mart logistic system combine to enable the company to master its strategic vision of a low-cost, friendly, and trustworthy retail system. Stalk et al. (1992: 58) explains:

> This strategic vision reached its fullest expression in a largely invisible logistics technique known as "cross-docking". In this system, goods are continuously delivered to Wal-Mart's warehouses, where they are selected, repacked, and then dispatched to stores, often without ever sitting in inventory. Instead of spending valuable time in the warehouse, goods just cross from one loading dock to another in 48 hours or less. Cross-docking enables Wal-Mart to achieve the economies that come with purchasing full truckloads of goods while avoiding the usual inventory and handling costs. Wal-

Mart runs a full 85% of its goods through its warehouse system—as opposed to only 50% for Kmart. This reduces Wal-Mart's costs of sales by 2% to 3% compared with the industry average.

Cross-docking is a material extension of the computerized information system on which it is based. Both systems are expensive, complex, and difficult to manage, integrating different, separate activities in the Wal-Mart value chain.

Let us summarize the strategic breakthrough achieved by Wal-Mart that became a new benchmark for the retail industry. First, the weakest competitor among the discount retailers in the 1960s and 1970s—in terms of resources and growth potential—became the strongest competitor. It matched competitors' moves one by one (for example, in terms of prices and sales techniques) while at the same time experimenting with industry's standard ways of doing business. One of Wal-Mart's early strategic decisions was to open stores in small towns ignored by competitors because of the high cost of entry and low predictions of cash flows. Wal-Mart was able to enter such towns because of its extraordinarily low costs.

Second, Wal-Mart always kept costs at an extremely low level compared with the industry average. From the beginning the company aimed at developing an effective, complex sociotechnical system that maintains low costs on a permanent basis. Today, Wal-Mart's "everyday low prices" are not a result of particularly fortunate purchasing or sophisticated promotion. They result from a dynamic logistics system called "cross-docking" that enables the control and cost containment of operations of the system as a whole, not of its individual parts.

Third, the system of capabilities developed by Wal-Mart is complex and difficult to imitate because: (1) it is built from many interrelated technical and social elements and processes diffused through the whole company; (2) it is expensive to set up quickly, as it extends into every part of the organization, and many of the support systems make sense only as a part of a total system and not as stand-alone investments; (3) its complexity and demand for high-speed management makes it difficult to manage even by Wal-Mart's well-trained, experienced, motivated workforce.

Finally, the diffused logistics of the procurement-inventory-replenishment system developed by Wal-Mart proved to be a unique strategic capability that can be used in new areas of competition. Wal-Mart's traditional competitor Kmart developed the idea of warehouse clubs, that is, special stores that sell products in huge quantities at an extremely low price. Wal-Mart only entered this market in 1983; however, four years later, its superb low-cost logistics permitted Wal-Mart to surpass all competitors and take the lead. Stalk et al. (1992) noted that Wal-Mart's strategic capabilities enabled the firm to repeat this rapid penetration strategy in numerous other U.S. retail sectors.

CRITICAL FACTORS IN BREAKTHROUGHS

We began this chapter by exploring the concept of the managerial breakthrough as a frame-breaking change that involves sharp and simultaneous shifts in strategy, power structure, and controls. Next, we introduced two crucial dimensions of breakthrough: the consumer/competitor thrust and focused/diffused scope. Then we explored four generic strategies guiding successful frame-breaking changes. Each of these strategies were illustrated by success stories of breakthroughs: Toyota's development of the Lexus car, The Body Shop International's management system, Catalina's computer system, and Wal-Mart's logistics. While each of these examples is unique, and the logic of breakthrough strategies is distinctive, the critical organizational adaptation factors are as follows:

1. Goal. The precise goal of the breakthrough must be established. Though seemingly obvious, goal clarification is especially important in managing breakthroughs. While organizations can be lucky and stumble upon major technological inventions or develop a new customer approach, such luck is not common. Therefore, frame-breaking change must have a simple but clear core concept, one that is easy to communicate and explain.

2. Organization. The idea of a breakthrough must be explicitly stated and tied to the organizational norms, values, and dreams. This communication should trigger the support of the organizational culture and challenge people's abilities and knowledge. All breakthroughs must penetrate the organization and build creative tension at the lower echelons of the organization, as did the technical and brand challenges of Lexus, new products and social concerns in The Body Shop, and the sophisticated logistics of Wal-Mart.

3. Leadership. The breakthrough required strong leadership from the top and direct involvement in the programs of action. Anita Roddick, Sam Walton, and the Lexus project leader, Ichiro Suzuki, provided direction and established priorities, contagious enthusiasm, support, and role models, all of which helped in implementing their breakthrough idea.

4. Ongoing. The new fit of strategy, structure, and controls must be achieved in the organization after the breakthrough becomes a "normal part" of organizational operations that should and can be improved over time. Each of the successful organizations described above have a unique "driver." In the case of Lexus the driver was a structurally separate organization and dealers network; in The Body Shop, on-going training; and at Wal-Mart, Sam Walton's personal leadership style.

EIGHT

Continuous Improvement Leadership Patterns

> Effective strategic managers seek to identify a few central themes that can help to draw diverse efforts together in a common cause. Once identified, these themes help to maintain focus and consistency in the strategy. They make it easier to discuss and monitor strategic thrusts. (Quinn 1980: 15)

In the preceding chapters we discussed in detail five components of the continuous improvement theory. We started our discussion in Chapter 1 by linking three processes: developing a competitive advantage; designing the value chain; and formulating a strategy. The cumulative goal of these processes was adaptation of the company to its environment. On this foundation we developed in Chapter 2 a theory of continuous improvement, which we enhanced in subsequent chapters along two dimensions: (1) from an internal to an external perspective that included the company's boundaries and external linkages, and (2) from simple to increasingly complex theoretical components. Thus, in Chapter 3 we started with the most basic element of the continuous improvement process: self-managed teams. In Chapter 4 we discussed more complex cross-functional teams, including their purpose, modes of operation, and various types. In the following chapter we covered the focus, strategies, and tools of benchmarking. Chapter 6 explained the complex issue of developing and sustaining linkages among organizations. Finally, Chapter 7 analyzed the use of breakthroughs for rejuvenating an organization's competitive advantage, its value chain, and the new logic and focus of an improvement program.

A common theme running throughout our discussion of the theory and practice of continuous improvement was the dramatic need for constant adaptation and innovation in order to ensure a company's long-term success. In this chapter we add a final element to our theory by explaining the role of the leadership in a world-class, continuously improving organization. In order to understand the importance and role of leadership in the continuous improvement process, we must understand the evolution of a dominant leadership pattern.

LEADERSHIP EVOLUTION

The traditional paradigm, that is, the model or pattern of leadership, in organizations during the last few decades was relatively simple and traditional. Leaders were charismatic managers who devised clever strategies and executed them effectively. The execution usually involved several compromises. To speed up innovations, organizations had to accept higher R&D costs; to expand market share, they had to cut prices and consequently their profit margin; to diversity in terms of products or markets they had to accept high transaction costs, high risk, and so forth. The leader of an organization had an unspoken agreement with his followers offering security and the prospect of a more rewarding future in return for their compliance and (sometimes) motivation.

Changes in the marketplace during the eighties and nineties rendered this pattern obsolete. As we have discussed throughout the book, a revolution has taken place in global markets. The process of globalization affects almost every corporation in the developed world through increased pressures of hostile competition and demanding customers. Modern telecommunications networks and computers transformed the workplace in terms of how people process information and learn and make decisions. Equally important, this modernization lowers the financial costs of communications and control. Organizations are learning how to increase quality while forcing costs down, as well as how to customize production lots and expand post-sale service. Many companies are experiencing the advantages and effectiveness of a multi-skilled, team-oriented workforce (Katzenbach and Smith

1993). These new developments have created a demand for a different kind of leadership. Organizations now require a heroic, transformational leader (Tichy and Devanna 1986).

The transformational leader revolutionizes and rejuvenates a company in three steps (Tichy 1993). First, he convinces the organization of the need for change, articulating why the change is necessary and dealing with initial resistance. Second, he directs the team effort to build a powerful vision of the company's future with employees sharing this vision. Third, he skillfully, often ruthlessly, manages the process to change the company's technical, social, and organizational architecture.

The model of a transformational leader was expanded during the last few years as some companies managed to move beyond the revolutionary stages to become continuously improving, world-class competitors. These companies and their leaders are not just the best in a regional market or product segment. They are transgressing typical market-product definitions and simply becoming global benchmarks. They fuse management and leadership in a dynamic learning mode that resolves tensions naturally occurring in organizations that punctuate constant improvement with periodic revolutionary change. The most typical tensions exist between (1) the needs of stability and change; (2) centralization and delegation and empowerment; and (3) the growing complexity of a system and the need for simple, transparent yet creative management.

The following sections discuss in detail the three-stage evolution from transactional to world-class leadership.

TRANSACTIONAL LEADER

Traditional concepts and practices of leadership have both their strengths and weaknesses, but are generally incongruent with continuous improvement theory and practice. Let us briefly review two traditional approaches to leadership and discuss why they do not answer the demands of today's marketplace. A number of approaches to leadership, both in theory and practice are based on a leader's access to the sources of power (French and Raven 1959). Traditionally, a leader's power base was secured by control of at least three sources of power: a formal position, a system of rewards and punishment, and information flows. Control over a formal position enabled the leader to establish chain of command and either to make most of the decisions alone or delegate them to subordinates. His control over rewards and punishment allowed the leader to influence subordinates' behavior. Control over information ensured the leader expert knowledge and a superior position due to the knowledge base. The practical strength of such an approach was evident. It allowed companies to build orderly organizational structures and execute standard procedures of action utilizing the advantages of specialization. The weakness of this leadership concept lay in the consolidation of bureaucratic structures, the lack of coordination, turf battles, low satisfaction, and poor performance. The negative effects of leadership based on access to power were described by Lee Iaccoca (1984).

After Iaccoca took over as CEO of the Chrysler Corporation in early 1979, he quickly noticed that noone was coordinating individual efforts. Neither managers nor workers focused on a company goal. There were thirty-five presidents in the company, each with his own purpose and method of operation. There were no identified contacts in the major departments. There was no system of teamwork and communication was poor. Everybody worked independently and attended to separate tasks. Designers and engineers developed cars without attention to the customers' needs; workers in the manufacturing area built cars with the hope that somebody from sales would eventually sell them. It is not surprising that Chrysler was on the brink of bankruptcy. Iaccoca summarized the whole picture in one word: "nightmare."

Another approach to leadership centers on individual traits and assumes that some people are more likely to become leaders than others (Bennis and Naums 1985). The core assumptions of this theory are that leaders have special, desirable traits, for example, oral communication skills, human relations skills, a need for career advancement, resistance to stress, tolerance of uncertainty and a lack of security, organizing and planning skills, energy, and flexibility. The major problem with this approach to leadership is that while such traits may be desirable, the way they are put into practice is much more important. If they are utilized within formal, centralized bureaucratic hierarchies, leaders possessing these traits may not perform better than others. Certainly IBM, General Motors, Sears, Westinghouse, Digital Equipment, and American Express were led by many individuals with these traits during the 1980s, and they still could not prevent financial and marketing problems from occurring in the beginning of the 1990s. In each of these cases, there are specific reasons for the company's downfall, such as market downturns, technological breakthroughs, and keen competition. However, the generic reason for their decline is the companies' lack of a clear vision and their inability to empower their employees to meet the demands of the marketplace. To meet these demands, a transformational kind of leadership slowly gained acceptance in the theory and business practices of the eighties.

TRANSFORMATIONAL LEADERSHIP

The Art of Revolutions

The new leadership approach that is indispensable in a volatile economic market recognizes the need for analyzing a company's strengths and weaknesses and for initiating revolutionary change that prepares a company to meet future challenges and demands. Thus, real transformational leaders not only adapt to change, but they learn and stay ahead of change. The transformational leadership concept restores the role of the organizational leader to a dominant position in two respects. First, the frame of reference of a transformational leader is a set of relentlessly followed core values or standards, such as success, integrity, respect, trust, and fairness (Kuhnert and Lewis 1987). Second, a transformational leader recognizes the need for a periodic reassessment of the assumptions regarding the organization's success. The test of transformational leadership is, therefore, a *successful management of organizational transformations* in order to cope with rapid environmental changes and to stay ahead of competitors. In short, transformational leaders break existing structures and constantly rebuild their organization. However, as Tushman, Newman, and Romanelli (1986) indicate, such leadership is rare. In their study of forty cases of revolutionary change, over 80 percent were accelerated by a financial crisis in which the CEO was replaced. Less than 20 percent of leaders recognized the need for rapid, revolutionary change.

Based on these findings (Cushman and King 1993; Hughes 1990; Kanter 1989), as well as on practical organizational applications, two core skill areas are generally recognized as requirements for transformational leadership: strategic and operational. The strategic aspect of transformational leadership requires that leaders, in anticipation of future demands and challenges, offer a clear vision of what the company must achieve and why, be consistent in this vision as long as it is relevant to market conditions, and immediately change the vision when it is no longer suitable. The operational aspect of leadership requires that managers master the skill of restructuring an organization and empowering the employees by building and coaching teams. Let us address each of these issues in turn.

Strategy: Development of a Vision

> The first and most crucial point to remember is that employees can't embrace the new strategy if they don't know what it is. (Fisher 1988: 42)

Many large companies operate without a clear strategy and vision of the future: their sheer size allows them to continue for a long period of time. However, they eventually run into trouble. The most obvious examples are furnished by three American giants: IBM, General Motors, and Sears. In retrospect, it is clear that these companies suffered from the lack of a corporate vision.

Transformational leaders offer a vision that is simple, inspiring and challenging.

Simple.   The vision must be simple for two reasons: (1) to make it understandable and measurable to employees, suppliers, customers and other stakeholders; and (2) to focus team efforts. When Gillette decided to develop a Sensor razor, management created a simple vision of a product that would be functional, easy to produce, and at the same time imaginative. This vision effectively focused the efforts of the team developing the parameters of the innovative Sensor razor. Being "functional" meant that it not only had to shave well, but also needed to fit easily in the user's hand and on the shelf for storage. Being "easy to produce" meant that the supply and production costs must be kept low. Finally, being "imaginative" meant that the product must convey a high-tech image, a difficult task for a product as standard as a razor. The vision proved to be successful. The Sensor razor was a market hit; later, Gillette developed another focused vision in creating the imaginative Sensor razor for women.

Inspiring. The vision must be inspiring to unleash teams members' creativity and to spark their motivation. Cindy Ransom became a Clorex hero after her plant in Fairfield, California was named the most improved in the company's household division (Dumaine 1993: 39). In 1990, she started with a vision of a continuous improvement program run primarily by workers. The task of redesigning and simplifying the company's operation proved to be inspiring and exciting to the workers, who established training programs, set out work rules, and finally reorganized the plant into five customer-oriented business units. While the employees concentrated on the internal improvements, top management improved linkages with suppliers and focused on customer needs.

Challenging. Finally, the vision must be challenging so that when pursued it helps the company to become equal to or better than its competitors and to differentiate its product from the myriad of other products on the market. Therefore the vision must be framed in such a way that the improvement program is punctuated with visible (even if small) successes, in order to keep management and employee involvement and motivation high. The visions of Lexus car, Body Shop business and social activities, and Wal-Mart discount and friendly stores (discussed in Chapter 7) are all skillfully framed in a way which constantly challenges all members of the organization.

Let us conclude with a vision of a company whose CEO mastered the art of simplicity, excitement, and challenge. John Welch, the CEO of General Electric, outlined his vision and its roots in a speech to GE stakeholders (Welch, 1988:2):

> Our experience during the late 70s in grappling with world competition etched very clearly on our minds the belief that companies that held on to marginal busi-nesses—or less than world-competitive operations of *any* sort—wouldn't be around for very long. That analysis led us to a strategy that said we had to be number one or number two in each of our businesses...or we had to see a way to get there...or exit if we couldn't...That was— that is—our strategy: simple, even stark.

Operations: Barrier Removal

Middle managers who master skills
such as team building and intrapre-
neurship and who acquire broad functional expertise will likely be in the
best position to bet tomorrow's top
corporate jobs. That's because the role
of the top executive is becoming more
like that of a team player and broker
of other's efforts, not that of an auto-
crat. (Dumaine: 1993: 39)

Ostroff and Smith (1992), two consultants at McKinsey and
Company, found that those organizations that responded
rapidly to successive transformational visions by altering and
elevating organizational performance were restructured by their
leaders in such a way as to make teams, not individuals, the
focus of performance. This major difference poses fundamen-
tally new challenges of leadership related to unique features of
effective teamwork. As we noted in Chapters 3 and 4, research
shows that effective teams have three major characteristics: (1)
mutually constructed and supported goals; (2) the integration of
team members' interests, concerns and contributions; and (3) a
culture of mutual respect, trust, and confidence. It follows from
these characteristics that the operational responsibility of the
leader is the removal of barriers that can hinder team performance in terms of tasks or values. In practical terms, a leader
guards the team's so-called "embeddedness" in the organization. His role is more that of a coach and facilitator than that of
a principal.

According to Cushman and King (1993), a team's embeddedness must be analyzed on task, social, and psychological
levels (Cohen 1969) that correspond to the three features of
effective teamwork.

Task Embeddedness.   Task embeddedness refers to the
following questions: What kind of task has the team been given?
How is the task integrated into the overall vision? How should

the results be evaluated? A leader must help develop tasks that are challenging and vision-relevant and at the same time remove all barriers that prevent team members from understanding and accepting their tasks. In practical terms this means that a transitional leader should be able to answer the following questions in the affirmative:

- Does the task relate to and help to achieve the overall vision?

- Is the task clearly understood, agreed upon, and accepted by all team members?

- Do team members have the skills necessary to accomplish the task?

- Is the task clearly measurable?

- Is a system in place to ensure quick feedback of results?

Social Embeddedness.   Social embeddedness refers to the following question: How do team values, norms, and rules of conduct relate to the company's values? Often companies create obvious discrepancies by trying to build teamwork and by advocating openness and innovation, while keeping rigid structures and control systems in place. One solution traditionally used to address this problem is the creation of a so-called "binary" organization. The old organization performs in the traditional ways, while teams operate in the new part, usually with a separate budget, different location, and different management practices, all of which ensure the teams' social embeddedness. In this way IBM developed its highly successful PC in the beginning of the 1980s, as well as Honda, its City car. However, this solution remains problematic because it isolates teamwork from normal operations and limits it to special projects. If the company embarks on a continuous improvement program, it must let the concept of teamwork permeate the organization as a whole. Leaders usually must adapt corporate values and norms to the realities of teamwork in order to ensure social embeddedness of teams.

Psychological Embeddedness.   Psychological embeddedness relates to the suitability of individual personalities within a given team. A leader must ensure the development of a culture of trust and respect through coaching members who experience difficulty in adapting to the team and removing them if necessary.

In practice, the concept of embeddedness must be applied to all five elements of the continuous improvement program and serve as an indicator of potential problems and barriers. Let us address each of the major challenges and problems of leadership that arise in the cases of self-managed teams, cross-functional teams, benchmarking, linkages, and breakthroughs.

Self-managed teams. These teams are created by people who know each other, and work in the same location. Often, the primary problem requiring assistance from the team leader is that of psychological embeddedness if team members do not communicate well and conflicts occur as a consequence. The leader must work as a moderator and facilitator until psychological and sociological embeddedness is achieved. However, the major problem of self-managed groups arises at the task level, because even medium-sized organizations find it difficult to connect operational tasks with organizational vision and strategy. Therefore, the crucial leadership challenge is to establish evident linkages between tasks performed at the team's level and general vision of the firm, in other words, to develop task embeddedness.

Cross-functional teams. Both the psychological and task embeddedness of cross-functional teams may pose problems; for instance, members of the team may not get along, or the task may seem vague at the beginning. The leadership challenge here is to create social embeddedness. Team members come from different departments; thus, their interests, concerns, and contributions are not usually (at the beginning) compatible. Members represent different subcultures of the organization. The leader's responsibility is to find and forge common values and norms in such teams, linking them with general corporate values.

Benchmarking. Benchmarking creates the combined challenge of task and social embeddedness. As we pointed out in Chapter 5, benchmarking fails when the team does not know exactly what to benchmark and how. The task, therefore, must be clearly defined, which determines its impact on effectiveness. Because a benchmarking team is usually cross-functional, leaders must also deal with the challenge of achieving social embeddedness.

Linkages and breakthroughs. Building linkages and managing breakthrough processes pose leadership challenges in all three areas: task, social, and psychological embeddedness, but for different reasons. In the case of linkages, the task is difficult to operationalize. Its content and form (that is, of linkages) change over time, as strategic partners' visions and strategies evolve. Social and psychological embeddedness creates challenges due to the clashing of different organizations' cultures, which must be negotiated and compromised at the same time that linkages are managed. In the case of breakthroughs, leaders face a challenge of creative destruction: tasks, values, and norms at the social, and to some extent, at the psychological level must develop and follow the general frame-breaking changes occurring within the organization. A system incorporating task, social, and psychological embeddedness must be dissolved to allow a new system to be built over time.

World-Class Leadership

Some companies have managed to go beyond the transformational pattern and develop themselves as world-class firms. World-class firms can be described as masters of both revolutionary changes and the continuous improvement process, and thus represent the best in the processes of learning and adaptation.

World-class leadership includes important elements of the transactional and transformational leadership pattern and more. To become a world-class leader, one must excel in the skills important to patterns shaping both forms of leadership. Similar to the transactional leader, the world-class leader is characterized by his ability to mobilize different power sources and to acquire and use personal skills to manage effectively within a given context. Like the transformational leader, the world-class leader must master the unique set of skills that lead to the art of context management necessary to build a vision and remove the internal barriers preventing people from adhering to that vision. But a world-class leader adds a new dimension in that he or she successfully manages the tensions occurring within companies that punctuate the continuous improvement process with frame-breaking changes.

As its foundation, continuous improvement requires a stable coalignment between an organization and its environment. However, frame-breaking changes implemented by transformational leaders destroy the coalignment, which typically creates three areas of tension: (1) the need for stability vs.

change; (2) centralization versus empowerment; and (3) the growing complexity of the system vs. the need for simple, transparent management.

Stability and Change Tension. Every organization needs stability in terms of repetitive procedures, structure, culture (norms and values), and marketing strategy in order to avoid chaos and create a measure of company effectiveness. This stability in world-class organizations is temporary, as the essence of environmental scanning and benchmarking lies in relentlessly searching for new ideas and solutions and implementing them before competitors. Therefore, the world-class leaders must, in the words of Hewlett-Packard Chairman and CEO Lewis Platt, practice preemptive self-destruction and renewal, and be willing as well to cannibalize effective organizational strategies and solutions while they are still successful and effective in order to ensure leadership in the future (Deutschman 1994). The danger of such constant destruction of organizational stability in search of forward adaptation lies in the production of inherent tension between the need for stability and change that can easily result from the degeneration of routines and values. The way in which world-class leaders address the tension between the simultaneous needs for stability and change is twofold.

Mission and Strategy. First, leaders build commitment around a compelling, shared mission and general strategies that can provide organizational members with a sense of directional stability during the frequent periods of organizational change. They anchor organizational stability in core norms and values instead of in structures or processes. Pharmaceutical giant Bristol-Meyers Squibb states its mission as "Number 1 by 2001"; IBM's famous mission statement is "IBM Means Service:"; the motto of toy producer Lego A/S is "Only the best is good enough"; and Federal Express states its mission as "Absolutely, Positively, Overnight." These slogans introduce a consistency in the company's general direction within a turbulent, risky environment.

Customer Focus. Second, world class leaders consistently make their company's customers a focus of the organization and its changes. As a result, this customer orientation becomes a stable frame of reference for both frame-breaking and incremental changes. Textile-maker Milliken & Co. became famous for its customer dedication in the market for towels, dust mops and similar products. Milliken provides its salespeople with up to 22 weeks of training sessions, after which the salespeople perform one year of on-the-job training. They are offered a myriad of support services, training, and computer links to maximize their responsiveness to their customers' special needs (Peters 1988). The company's customer-based focus is guarded by the company leader, as it is in every world-class organization.

Centralization and Empowerment Tension.   The second tension managed by a world-class leader is a centralization versus empowerment tension. The effective management of a world-class organization demands control over the organizational value chain in order to ensure the quick execution of planned change and to minimize the time lag between actions and results. At the same time, building the teams' embeddedness demands decentralization. The teams must share ownership of the problems and solutions, built commitment and involvement in the development of a vision, maintain effective communication, and ensure the prompt use of recognition and rewards.

Organizational members can anchor their needs for stability in a vision and customer focus only if those needs are widely shared. Achieving this level of support requires decentralization to enhance innovation, participation, and motivation. The world-class leader answers the simultaneous need of centralization and decentralization through a system of strict performance targets and creative human resource management.

World-class leaders establish strict performance targets for each of the organizational units. While tactical errors and mistakes are accepted, failure to meet targets is not. In this way, leaders centralize the targets and execution of goals, and at the same time provide units with the power to decide on all other issues. This approach is especially visible in the severe target demands imposed by Jack Welch at General Electric, where his lack of tolerance for failure earned him the name "Neutron Jack." At the same time, Jack Welch wholeheartedly supports the central theme of empowerment: ownership of the business. Ownership in this sense means that people further down the organizational ladder have the power to make and carry out all decisions.

Creative human resource management is indispensable for creating a climate of continuous learning and providing employees with the skills needed for good team performance and innovative problem solving. An interesting example is Korea's most successful *cheabol* (conglomerate): Samsung. In order to facilitate the transformation of Samsung's centralized management and obedience-oriented culture, the new chairman, Lee Kun-Hee, concurrently established new and challenging performance targets while launching a creative human resource development program. The program consists of several elements.

First, the company conducts intensive, often round-the-clock sessions for senior executives covering the issues of competitiveness, quality, and marketing of Samsung products, The meetings occur in different parts of the world and are videotaped and circulated throughout the company.

Second, all 850 top executives attend the "CEO School." The School consists of six months of training, three of which take place in Korea. The other three months of training are conducted overseas in order to learn a foreign language and experience other cultures. While abroad, executives are instructed to travel by car, bus, or train to see and understand the peculiarities of other countries.

The third element of this program is a regional specialist program for middle managers. Each year, about 400 managers are provided with funds and instructed to go abroad for one year to do whatever they choose. This "goof around and learn" program is a creative approach to the managers' development and enables Samsung to build a cadre of 2,000 managers who possess an intimate knowledge of other countries' languages and culture. The program will last for five years and cost about $100 million.

Finally, in order to enhance employees' problem-solving skills, Samsung allows some teams to study any subject or problem and try to solve it. The so called "techno-valleys" program has already produced a best-selling book entitled, "The PC is My Friend," as well as a new marketing strategy for selling televisions in Mexico.

Complexity and Simplicity Tension. Complexity is the major feature of a world-class organization that succeeds in adapting to its turbulent environment. This complexity has technological, structural, personnel, and strategic dimensions. Technological improvements and occasional breakthroughs increase the complexity of the organization's technology. The need to manage functions and processes of the value chain increases the organization's structural complexity. The pressures caused by frequent change and strict performance targets drain the psychological resources of an organization. Adaptive changes in strategy force subsequent changes throughout the organization in order to ensure a new level of coalignment. The high speed of all of these processes increases the complexity and decreases the lucidity of an organization. At the same time, the stakeholders, that is, competitors, customers, managers, employees, owners, regulators, and so forth, demand simplicity in the organization's structures and processes. The solution applied by world-class leaders to this tension is that of a network organization and open communications.

Network Organization. A network organization outsources those activities that can be performed more quickly, effectively, or cheaply by others. World-class leaders concentrate the company's performance on those functions for which the company has or can develop expert skills, that is, core competencies and capabilities. In the process of making itself more lean, the company simplifies its competitive posture. Hence, its stakeholders' attention can be focused on the most important processes to sustain core competencies.

Open Communication. The principle of open communications prompts top management to share the corporation's vision, goals, values, and other important information with stakeholders such as employees, vendors, and customers. Percy Barnevik of ABB summarizes the precept succinctly (Taylor 1991: 104): "Communications. I have no illusions about how hard it is to communicate clearly and quickly to tens of thousands of people around the world...If we in the executive committee could connect with all of them or even half of them and get them moving in roughly the same direction, we would be unstoppable. But it's enormously difficult." To solve this problem of communication, Barnevick argues that its management must over-inform its employees by sending the same messages through duplicate channels in ABB's matrix structure. In addition, the company's top managers hold frequent meetings with managers at all levels to communicate a common, repetitive message.

A FINAL WORD

Let us rephrase at a more general level what we established in our discussion of leadership patterns. Subtle, but important, distinctions exist among transactional, transformational, and world-class leaders. Each subsequent type of leader encompasses the most important attributes of the former type. Skillful management of organizational transactions has become a prerequisite for strong leaders, who must deal simultaneously with two general dimensions of leadership: task and sociopsychological (Blake and Morton 1978). Effective transformational leadership skills have become a cost of entry into the turbulent marketplace. World-class leaders meet the real challenges of managing paradoxes and tensions created by high-speed competition in the global marketplace. They are involved in an ongoing search for the balance between values and numbers. The tension is well-illustrated by a recent statement made by Jack Welch of GE in the company's 1992 annual report. He sketched two dimensions of leadership: following through on committments (financial or otherwise) and sharing the values of the company. He also described four types of leaders.

The first type of leader meets commitments and adheres to GE values: empowering and energizing company employees; focusing on the customer; resisting bureaucracy; cutting across boundaries; thinking globally; and holding the first or second global position in all its businesses. This type of person is a real leader at General Electric, one whose abilities are renowned among American companies and headhunters.

The second type of leader does not meet commitments and does not share values. General Electric parts with such leaders immediately.

The third type of leader fails to fulfill commitments but shares the company values. According to Jack Welch, he or she deserves a second chance, preferably in a different environment.

Finally, there are the old type of leaders: they deliver on commitments but do not share General Electric's current values. Welch (1992) comments:

And perhaps this type was more acceptable in easier times, but in an environment where we must have every good idea from every man and woman in the organization, we cannot afford management styles that suppress and intimidate. Whether we can convince and help these managers to change—recognizing how difficult that can be—or part company with them if they cannot, will be the ultimate test of our commitment to the transformation of this company and will determine the future of the mutual trust and respect we are building.

General Electric is a company used often as an example throughout this book, because GE skillfully manages frame-breaking changes and continuous improvement practices. The company established self-managed and cross-functional teams, molding them into an innovative Work-Out system. It bench-marks internally and externally, and skillfully builds linkages all over the world. However, Welch's statement indicates that GE decided to breakthrough in order to achieve a new level of improvement. As he pointed out, leadership is the key.

Notes

CHAPTER 1

1. M. Porter's concept of an organization as a value chain, to be discussed in chapter 3, effectively utilizes this distinction.

2. In chapter 2 we define capabilities more broadly as a set of processes in a strategic sense.

CHAPTER 2

3. For examples see Stewart (1991) on GE, Reid (1990) on Harley-Davidson, and Kapstein and Hoerr (1989) on Volvo.

4. The authors analyzed six significant strategic capabilities: relative size, relative market share, breadth of product lines, technological sophistication of manufacturing, managerial capabilities, and relative labor costs.

5. The only exceptional capability was the dominant European market share of the "European pooling bloc," which was natural, as this bloc consisted of six leading European producers.

6. This system is discussed in greater detail in chapter 5.

7. The nature, scope and function of QCs are discussed in detail in chapter 6.

8. The differences are well summarized in the HBS case study No. 9–687–011: "A Note of Quality: The Views of Deming, Juran and Crosby," Harvard Business School, Boston, Mass., 1986.

CHAPTER 4

9. This section is based upon M. Hardaker's and B. K. Ward's article, "How to Make Teams Work," *Harvard Business Review*, November-December 1987: 112–19.

CHAPTER 5

Portions of this chapter were taken from Cushman, D. P., and King, S. S. (1985), *Communication and High-Speed Management* (Albany, New York: SUNY Press).

CHAPTER 8

10. Europe market shares are limited by the quotas that allow Japanese producers to control very limited market shares, for example, 1 percent in Italy, 3 percent in France, up to 10 percent (in the United Kingdom).

References

ABB, 1991. *The Art of Being Local Worldwide*. Zurich: ABB Marketing Services.

———, 1989. *Six Months Report*. Zurich: ABB.

Abramis, D. J. 1990. Semi-conductor Manufacturing Team. Hackman, J. R. (ed). *Groups That Work*. San Francisco, Oxford: Jossey-Bass Publishers: 449–70.

Adam, E. E. 1991. Quality Circle Performance, *Journal of Management* 17, 25–39.

Adams, J. L. 1974. *Conceptual Blockbusting*. New York: Norton.

Altany, D. 1991. Share and Share, *Industry Week*, vol. 240, no. 14, July 15: 12–17.

Ancona, D. G. and Nadler, D. A. 1989. Top Hats and Executive Tales: Designing the Senior Team. *Sloan Management Review*, Fall: 19–28.

Ansoff, H. I., 1965. Concept of Strategy. In: J. B. Quinn, Mintzberg H. and James R. M. (eds). *The Strategy Process: Concepts, Contexts and Cases*. Englewood Cliffs, N.J.: Prentice-Hall.

Arbose, J. 1988. ABB - The New Energy Powerhouse. *International Management* June: 24–30.

Baning, K., and Wintermantel, D. 1991. Motorola Turns Vision into Profits. *Personel Journal* February: 51–55.

Barrett, F. D. 1987. Teamwork: How to Expand its Power and Punch. *Business Quarterly* 52 (3): 24–31.

Barry, D. 1991. Managing Bossless Teams: Lessons in Distributed Leadership. *Organizational Dynamics* 20 (1): 31–47.

Bennis, W. and B. Naums. 1985. *Leaders*. New York: Harper and Row.

Benson, T. E. 1992. IQS Defines the Goal. *Industry Week*, January 20: 28–30.

Blake, R., and J. Mouton. 1978. *The New Management Grid*, Howton: Gulf Publishing.

Bolman, L. G. and Deal, T. E. 1992. What Makes a Team Work?, *Organizational Dynamics* 2: 34–44.

Bonoma, T. V. 1984. *Managing Marketing*. New York: The Free Press.

Britain's Most Admired Companies. *The Economist*, 17th October 1992: 79–80.

Bunning, R. L., and Althisar, R. S. 1990. Modules: A Team Model for Manufacturing. *Personnel Journal*, March: 90–96.

Burlingham, B., 1990, This Woman Has Changed Business Forever, *Inc.*, June: 34–47.

Bylinsky, G. 1990. Company in Japan. *Fortune*, January 1: 83–88.

Cavaleri, S. and Obloj, K. 1993. *Management Systems: A Global Perspective*. Belmont, Calif.: Wadsworth.

Chandler, A., 1962. *Strategy and Structure*. Cambridge, Mass: MIT Press.

Chevron Set to Combine Five Units. 1992. *The New York Times*, Tuesday, June 2: D5.

Clare, D. A. and Sanford, D. G. 1984. Cooperation and Conflict Between Industrial Sales and Production. *Industrial Marketing Management* 13: 163–69.

Cohen, B. P., and X. Zhan. 1991. Status Processes in Enduring Work Groups. *American Sociological Review* 56: 79–88.

Connor, W. D. and Ploszajski, P. (eds). 1992. Escape from Socialism. Warsaw: IFIS Publishers.

Cushman, D. 1993. When Is Teamwork a Good and When Is It a Bad Solution to Organizational Problems. SUNY-Albany: *mimeo*.

———, and King, S. 1993. *High Speed Management: a Revolution in Organizational Communication in the 90s*. In S. Deetz (ed.), *Communication Yearbook*, 16: 209–237.

—— and King, S. S. (1995). *Communication and High-Speed Management.* Albany, N.Y.: SUNY Press.

Cusumano, M. A. 1988. Manufacturing Innovation: Lessons From the Japanese Auto Industry. *Sloan Management Review,* Fall: 29–39.

Deming, W. E. 1982. *Quality, Productivity and Competitive Position.* Cambridge, Mass.: Massachusetts Institute of Technology Center for Advanced Engineering Study.

——. 1986. *Out of the Crisis.* Cambridge, Mass: Massachusetts Institute of Technology Center for Advanced Engineering Study.

Denton, K. D. 1992. Building a Team. *Quality Progress,* October: 87–91.

Deschamps, J. P. and Nayak, P. R. 1992. Competing Through Products: Lessons from the Winners. *The Columbia Journal of World Business,* Summer: 38–54.

Deutschman, A. 1994. How H–P Continues to Grow and Grow, *Fortune,* May 2: 60–63.

Drucker, P. 1992. *Managing for the Future.* New York, Dutton.

Dulworth, M. R., Landen D. L., and Usilaner B. L. 1990. Employee Involvement Systems in U. S. Corporations: Right Objectives, Wrong Strategies. *National Productivity Review* 9 (2): 141–56.

Dumaine, B. 1993. The New Non-Manager Managers, *Fortune,* February 22: 38–42.

——. 1990. Who Needs a Boss. *Fortune.* May 7: 52–60.

Eisenstat, R. A. 1990. Compressor Team Start-Up. Hackman, J. R. (ed). *Groups That Work.* San Francisco, Oxford: Jossey-Bass Publishers: 411–26.

Fisher, A. B. 1988. The Downside of Downsizing. *Fortune,* 117: 42–52.

Flynn, J. 1991. Continuous Improvement: Application at General Electric. Student paper, Albany University.

Flynn, J. M. and Carè, F. (1994). *High-Speed Management and Continuous Improvement: Teamwork Applications at General*

Electric. In King, S. S. and Cushman, D. P. (eds). *High-Speed Management and Organizational Communication in the 1990s: A Reader.* Albany, N.Y.: SUNY Press.

French, J. R. P., and B. Raven. 1959. The Basis of Social Power. D. Cartwright, (ed). *Studies in Social Power.* Ann Arbor: Michigan Institute for Social Research.

Fuchsberg, G. 1992. Quality Programs Show Shoddy Results. *Wall Street Journal,* May 14: B1, B7.

Garvin, D. A. 1984. Japanese Quality Management. *The Columbia Journal of World Business* vol. 14, no. 3: 3–12.

Ginett, R. C. 1990. Airline Cockpit Crew. Hackman, J. R. (ed.), *Groups That Work.* San Francisco, Oxford: Jossey-Bass Publishers: 427–46.

Gupta, A. K., and Wilemon, D. 1988. The Credibility Cooperation Connection at the R & D - Marketing Interface. *Journal of Product Innovation Management* 5: 20–31.

Guterl, F. V. 1989. Goodbye Old Matrix. *Business Month,* February: 32–36.

Hackman, J. R. (ed). 1990. *Groups That Work.* San Francisco, Oxford: Jossey-Bass Publishers.

———, and Oldham, G. R. 1980. *Work Redesign.* Reading, Mass.: Addison Wesley.

———, Oldham, G. R., Janson R., & Purdy K. 1975. A New Strategy for Job Enrichment. *California Management Review* 17 (4): 55–71.

Hall, R. 1992. The Strategic Analysis of Intangible Resources, *Strategic Management Journal* 13 (2): 135–44.

Hambrick, D. C. and D'Aveni, R. A. 1988. Large Corporate Failures as Downward Spirals, *Administrative Science Quarterly 33*: 1–23.

Hardaker, M. and Ward, B. K. 1987. How to Make Team Work, *Harvard Business Review,* November-December: 112–19.

Hickman, C. R., and Silva M. A. 1987. *The Future 500: Creating Tomorrow's Organizations Today.* New York: NAL Books.

Hill, R. C., and Freedman S. M. 1992. Managing the Quality Process: Lessons From a Baldrigde Award Winner: A Conversation with John W. Wallace, Chief Executive Officer of the Wallace Company. *Academy of Management Executive* 6 (1): 76–89.

Hot Products. *Business Week*, June 7, 1993: 54–70.

House, C. H., and Price, R. L. 1991. The Return Map: Tracking Product Teams. *Harvard Business Review*, January-February: 92–100.

Hughes, G. D. 1990. Managing High-tech Product Cycles. *Academy of Management Executive* 4: 44–55.

Iacocca, L., and W. Novak. 1984. *Iacocca: An Autobiography*. New York: Bantam Books.

Imai, M. 1986. *Kaizen: The Key to Japan's Competitive Success.* New York: Random House.

Ishikawa, K. 1976. *Guide to Quality Control.* Tokyo: Asian Productivity Organization.

———. 1985. Principles of QC Circles Activities and Their Effects on Productivity in Japan: A Corporate Analysis. *Management International Review* 25 (3): 33–39.

Itami, H., with Roehl, T. H. 1987. *Mobilizing Invisible Assets*, Cambridge, Mass.: Harvard University Press.

Ju, Y. and Cushman, D. *Teamwork from a High Speed Management Perspective.* Albany, N.Y.: SUNY Press.

Kanter, R. M. 1989. The New Managerial Work. *Harvard Business Review* 67: 72–85.

Kapstein, J. and Hoerr J. 1989. Volvo's Radical New Plant: The Death of the Assembly Line? *Business Week*, August 29: 92–93.

Kathawala, Y. 1989. A Comparative Analysis of Selected Approaches to Quality. *International Journal of Quality and Reliability Management* 6 (5): 7–17.

Katzenbach, J. R., and D. K. Smith. *The Wisdom of Teams.* Boston, Mass.: Harvard Business School Press.

King, S., and Cushman, D. 1994. *High-Speed Management: Organizational Communication in the 1990's: A Reader.* Albany, N.Y.: SUNY Press.

Kinlaw, D. C. 1991. *Developing Superior Work Teams.* San Diego Cal.: Lexington Books, University Associates, Inc.

Knight, Ch. F. 1992. Emerson Electric: Consistent Profits, Consistently, *Harvard Business Review,* January-February: 57–70.

Kozminski, A. K. 1993. *Catching Up.* Albany, N.Y.: SUNY Press.

Krafcik, J. F. 1989. A New Diet for U. S. Manufacturing, *Technology Review,* January: 17–18.

Kuhnert, K. W., and Lewis, P. 1987. Transactional and Transformational Leadership: a Constructive/Development Analysis. *Academy of Management Review* 12 (4): 648–75.

Kupfer, A. 1991. The Champ of Cheap Clones. *Fortune.* September 23: 115–20.

Lawler, E. E., and Mohram S. A. 1985. Quality Circles: After the Fad, *Harvard Business Review,* January-February: 65–71.

Magjuka, R. J. 1991/1992. Survey: Self Managed Teams Achieve Continuous Improvement Best. *National Productivity Review,* Winter: 51–57.

Meyer, M. W. and Zucker, L. G. 1989. *Permanently Failing Organizations.* London: Sage.

Miles, R. E., and Snow, C. E. 1986. Organizations: New Concepts for New Forms. *California Management Review* XXVIII (3), Spring: 62–73.

Miller, D., and Friesen, P. 1984. Organizations: A Quantum View, Englewood Cliffs, N.J.: Prentice-Hall.

Moen, R. D., Nolan, T. W., and Provost, L. P. 1991. Improvement of Quality. In *Improving Quality Through Planned Experimentation.* New York: McGraw-Hill: 1–23.

Mohr, W. L. and Mohr, H. 1983. *Quality Circles: Changing Imagers of People at Work.* Reading, Mass.: Addison Wesley Publishing Co.

Moskel, B. S. 1991. Is Industry Ready for Adult Relationships. *Industry Week*, January 21: 18–25.

Nelson, R., 1991. On the Public and Private Elements of Technology. New York: Columbia University, *mimeo*.

———, and Winter, S. G. 1982. *An Evolutionary Theory of Economic Change*. Cambridge, Mass.: Harvard University Press.

Niland, P., 1989. U.S.-Japanese Joint Venture—New United Motor Manufacturing Inc. (NUMMI) *Planning Review*, January-February.

Nohria, N., and Garcia-Pont C. 1991. Global Strategic Linkages and Industry Structure. *Strategic Management Journal* 12 (1): 105–24.

Nonaka, I. 1988. Toward Middle-Up-Down Management: Accelerating Information Creation. *Sloan Management Review*, Spring, 29 (3): 9–18.

O'Brien, S. 1989. Albany International Strongly Positioned Globally for the 90-ties. *Paperage*, September: 13–17.

Obloj, K. and Davis, A. S. 1991. Innovation without Change: The Contradiction between Theories-Espoused and Theories-in-Use. *Journal of Management Studies* 28 (4): 323–38.

Ohmae, K. 1989. The Global Logic of Strategic Alliances. *Harvard Business Review* 89 (2): 143–54.

Patten, T. H. 1991/92. Beyond Systems—The Politics of Managing in a TQM Environment. *National Productivity Review*, Winter: 9–19.

Paulsen, K. M. 1989. Use Gain-sharing to Build a Winning Team. *Supervision*, April: 17–19.

Perrow, Ch. 1992. Review of the M. Best "The New Competition: Institutions of Industrial Restructuring," *Administrative Science Quarterly*, March: 162–66.

Perry, N. J. 1991. The Workers of the Future. *Fortune*, Spring/Summer: 68–72.

Peters, T. 1991b. Get Innovative or Get Dead (Part Two). *California Management Review* 33 (2): 9–23.

Peters, T. 1991a. Get Innovative or Get Dead (Part One). *California Management Review* 33 (1): 9–26.

Philips, M. E., Goodman, R. A., and Sackman, S. A. 1992. Exploring the Complex Cultural Milieu of Project Teams. UCLA (mimeo).

Pinto, M. B., and Pinto, J. K. 1990. Project Team Communication and Cross-Functional Communication in New Program Development. *Journal of Product Innovation Management* 7: 200–212.

Porter, M. 1985. *Competitive Advantage*. New York: The Free Press.

———. 1980. *Competitive Strategy*. New York: The Free Press.

Prahalad, C. K., and Hamel, G. 1990. The Core Competence of the Corporation, *Harvard Business Review*, May-June: 79–91.

Rawlinson, J. G. 1981. *Creative Thinking and Brainstorming*. New York: Halsted Press.

Ohmae, K. 1982. *The Mind of the Strategist*. New York: McGraw-Hill.

Ohmae, K. 1988. Getting Back to Strategy, *Harvard Business Review*, November-December: 149–56.

Peters, T. 1988. *Thriving on Chaos*. London: MacMillan.

Peters, T. J., and Waterman, R. H. 1982. *In Search of Excellence*. New York: Harper & Row.

Pont, O., Cary, U., Kelley, K., and Forrest, F. 1992. Quality, *Business Week*, November 30: 66–74.

Quinn, J. B. 1980. Managing Strategic Change. *Sloan Management Review* 21 (4): 3–20.

Reid, P. C. 1990. *Well Made in America: Lessons from Harley-Davidson on Being the Best*. New York: McGraw-Hill.

Rockart, J., and Short, J. 1989. IT in the 1990's: Managing Organizational Interdependencies. *Sloan Management Review* 30: 7–17.

Rohan, T. M. 1990. New Crisis in Quality. *Industry Week*, October 15: 11–14.

Rumelt, R. 1987. Theory, Strategy, and Entrepreneurship. Teece, D. J. (ed). *The Competitive Challenge*. New York: Harper and Row.

Sam Walton in His Own Words. *Fortune*. June 29, 1992: 98–106.

Sasaki, T. 1991. How the Japanese Accelerated New Car Development, *Long Range Planning* vol. 24, No. 1: 15–25.

Schafer, R. H., and Harvey, A. T. 1992. Successful Change Programs Begin with Results. *Harvard Business Review*, January-February: 80–89.

Scholtes, P. R. 1988. *The Team Handbook*. Madison, Wis.: Joiner Associates Inc.

Senge, P. 1990. *The Fifth Discipline*. New York: Doubleday.

Slatter, S. 1986. Corporate Recovery. Harmondsworth, Middlesex: Penguin Books.

Staff, I. 1990. Albany International Empowers its People to Meet its the 90-ties. *American Papermaker*, September: 63.

Stalk, G., Evans, P., and Shulman, L. E. 1992. Competing on Capabilities: The New Rules of Corporate Strategy. *Harvard Business Review*, March-April: 57–69.

Stevick, L. 1990. Preventing Process Problems. *Quality Progress*. September: 66–73.

Stewart, T. A. 1991. GE Keeps Those Ideas Coming. *Fortune*, August 12: 41–49.

———. 1992. The Search for the Organization of Tomorrow. *Fortune*, May 18: 93–98.

Taylor, A. 1990. Why Toyota Keeps Getting Better and Better All the Time. *Fortune*, November 19: 66–79.

———. 1989. Here Come Japan's New Luxury Cars. *Fortune*, August 14: 62–66.

Taylor, W. 1991. The Logic of Global Business—An Interview With ABB's Percy Barnevik. *Harvard Business Review*, March-April: 91–105.

Tichy, N. M. 1993. *Control Your Destiny or Someone Else Will.* New York: Doubleday/Currency.

————, and Devannba, M. A. The Transformational Leader. *Training and Development Journal* 40 (7): 27–32.

Tushman, M. L., Newman, W. H., and Romanelli, E. 1986. Convergence and Upheaval: Managing the Unsteady Pace of Organizational Evolution. *California Management Review* XXIX (1): 29–44.

Verespej, M. A. 1990. When you Put the Team in Charge. *Industry Week,* December 3: 30–32.

Vessey, J. T. 1991. The New Competitors: They Think in Terms of Speed to Market. *Academy of Management Executive* (5) 2: 23–33.

Walker, R. 1992. Rank Xerox—Management Revolution. *Long Range Planning* 25 (1): 9–21.

Walton, M. 1990. *Deming Management at Work.* New York: G. P. Putnam's Sons.

————. 1986. *The Deming Management Method.* New York: Perigee.

Watanabe, S. 1991. The Japanese Quality Circle: Why It Works. *International Labor Review* 130 (1): 57–80.

Welch, J. 1988. Managing For the Nineties. *GE Executive Speech Reprint.* Presented at the General Electric Annual Meeting of Share Owners. Waukesha, Wisconsin, April 27.

————. 1992. Statement in the Annual Report: Excerpt quoted under the title: "A Balance Between Values and Numbers." *The New York Times,* March 4: D–1.22.

Wellins, R., and George, J. 1991. The Key to Self-directed Teams. *Training and Development Journal* 45 (4): 26–31.

Williams, J. R. 1992. How Sustainable is Your Competitive Advantage. *California Management Review* 34 (3).

Womack, J. P., Jones D. T., and Ross D. 1990. *The Machine That Changed the World.* New York: Macmillan.

Work-Out. 1991. Crotonville: General Electric.

Index